"Douglas Wilson has a legendary track record of helping reintroduce his audience to the great Christian intellectual tradition. In *Writers to Read*, we find Wilson at his best: curating the authors who have inspired him and who he believes will galvanize the next generation with theological conviction and imagination. Highly recommended."

Gregory Alan Thornbury, President, The King's College; author, *Recovering Classic Evangelicalism*

"If you combined G. K. Chesterton, H. L. Menken, and P. G. Wodehouse and mixed them with evangelicalism, you'd produce a writer like Douglas Wilson. Not only is Wilson one of our finest writers; he's a superb reader and an excellent guide to the writing of luminaries such as Chesterton, Menken, and Wodehouse. Whether introducing you to authors you've never read or reacquainting you with old favorites, *Writers to Read* will help you become a better reader."

Joe Carter, Senior Editor, Acton Institute; co-author, *How to Argue Like Jesus*

"Wilson opens the twentieth-century vault to reveal a collection of authors who lived during our memory, or our grandparents', and are worthy companions on the shelf with Lewis and Tolkien. Refreshingly broad, Wilson connects you personally with nine authors and critiques them with the penetrating Christian perspective present in all of Wilson's works. This is a must-read for those who, like me, appreciate a few contemporary stepping-stones between Lewis and the great books of antiquity."

David Goodwin, President, Association of Classical Christian Schools

"Too many books celebrate great literature without answering the one question we all ask: Why? Why are some authors great? Readers want to know just as much as writers, and Douglas Wilson takes up this question as a humble student of nine skilled prose artists. He has studied their lives and analyzed their works and here offers several of his key discoveries. *Writers to Read* is a valuable education. Even more, it is an entertaining frolic through literature you do not want to miss."

Tony Reinke, Staff Writer and Researcher, Desiring God Ministries; author, *Lit!: A Christian Guide to Reading Books*

"Doug Wilson is regarded by both friends and foes as a master wordsmith. In *Writers to Read*, he introduces us to those who taught him (and still teach him) his craft. This book is like a side door into a little diner down a back alley where the nouns pop, the verbs sizzle, and the fry cooks are known only by their initials. If you want an inside look at the art of word weaving, this book is for you."

Joe Rigney, Assistant Professor of Theology and Christian Worldview, Bethlehem College and Seminary; author, *The Things of Earth* and *Live Like a Narnian*

WRITERS TO READ

WRITERS

TO

READ

Nine Names That Belong
on Your Bookshelf

DOUGLAS WILSON

WHEATON, ILLINOIS

Trade paperback ISBN: 978-1-4335-4583-2
ePub ISBN: 978-1-4335-4586-3
PDF ISBN: 978-1-4335-4584-9
Mobipocket ISBN: 978-1-4335-4585-6

Library of Congress Cataloging-in-Publication Data
Wilson, Douglas.
   Writers to read : nine names that belong on your bookshelf / Douglas Wilson.
      pages cm
   Includes bibliographical references and index.
   ISBN 978-1-4335-4583-2 (tp)
     1. Literature—Philosophy. 2. Best books. 3. Books and reading. I. Title.
PN49.W56   2015
801—dc23   2015003989

Crossway is a publishing ministry of Good News Publishers.

VP		25	24	23	22	21	20	19	18	17	16	15
15	14	13	12	11	10	9	8	7	6	5	4	3	2	1

For Shadrach, and the lifetime
of reading before you.

Contents

Introduction

Samuel Johnson once said that no one but a blockhead ever wrote but for money. But leaving aside such a base calumny on my possible motives, the main argument will be that if books are among our friends, we ought to apply similar standards to them that we apply to our flesh-and-blood friends. We should want to choose them wisely and well and hope that we will be the better for their companionship.

In this book I would like to introduce you to a few of my close friends, suggesting nine names that belong on your bookshelf. Some have been my friends from childhood, some for many years, and one I met just recently. The best thing about these friendships is that most of them have or had no idea that I exist.

There is one curiosity about them: a number of years ago, I noticed that I tended to gravitate toward friends who, in the form in which we meet them, are largely characterized on book covers by initials instead of their first names—C. S., P. G., G. K, J. R. R., and T. S. Be that as it may, I want to introduce you. We may not get to the point where we call anyone "Plum" or "Jack," but that should be no barrier to this sort of friendship.

If you are already acquainted with these writers, as a number of you undoubtedly are, then perhaps we can remind one another of stories, the way friends often do in the absence of another. Then there was a time . . .

Often the friends of writers are writers themselves, and so as iron sharpens iron, a writing friend makes a fellow writer sharpen his pencil. But it need not be that way. A writer needs friends who simply benefit from knowing him, which is another way of saying that good writers need good readers. And just as writers need to work at it to write well, so also readers should work at it in order to be able to read well.

My hope in this book of introduction is to help us all become better readers of some fine writers. Quoting Samuel Johnson again, what is written without effort is usually read without pleasure—but it goes the other way as well. What is read without honest effort is written in vain, and these are writers of a caliber that should never receive that kind of an insult.

Some emphasis here and there is placed on those writers and aspiring writers who want to have their outlook on the world, and their resultant writing, shaped by these literary friendships. Good writers never tire of seeking out ways to develop their skills, and I trust this book may prove to be a help in that regard. He who walks with the wise will be wise. He who reads good writing will come to know what good writing is. For those who wish to become better writers, I hope to explain in the course of this book why anyone who wants to write well should return to these authors again and again. They should be regular companions. The argument will be that books that pass the test that Lewis poses in *An Experiment in Criticism* should be a book that helps writers hone their craft. But this is *not* just a book for writers—though I hope writers may profit from it.

Good readers do more than just sit slack-jawed. They learn something of the craft of writing, if only to understand and appreciate what they are reading. Reading and writing constitute a conversation, and the point should always be to have an *intelligent* conversation, whether or not one of the parties intends to go off and repeat—as a writer himself—what he has heard. An intelligent conversation should be able to stand or fall on its own, whether or not it is repeated or continued somewhere else.

I have adopted the very straightforward arrangement of treating all these authors in the order of their births. Treating them chronologically in this fashion will take us from G. K. Chesterton, who was born in 1874—when Jesse James was still robbing trains—to N. D. Wilson, who was born in 1978, just over a century later, long after Jesse James quit doing anything of the kind. But taking an opportunity that may not pass by this way again, I should point out that Wilson had a great-great-granduncle, Jesse James Wilson, who was named for that famous outlaw. And . . . where was I?

For the most part, these writers straddle the twentieth century. Some of them started in the latter part of the nineteenth, and at the time of my writing, we are now just fourteen years into the twenty-first. Not only do these writers straddle the twentieth century, but they represent it rather well.

It is often said that classic books, and classic authors, are measured by what is called "the test of time." This is quite right and pretty obvious when we are dealing with the classics of three centuries ago. If books survive down to the present day, with people still reading them, then it is not foolish to presume that they probably have something going for them. Using a phrase from the Darwinists, adapted for our own purposes, there is a sense in which we are witnessing the survival of the fittest. They are classics because they are still in the curriculum. They are classics because they are still going strong.

But when we are considering books that were written in our own century, we have a completely different perspective because we do not yet know which books will stand that test of time. The classics that our generation produced emerged in the midst of a great crowd of clutter, and the clutter is just as obvious to us as the future classics are—and we don't rightly know which ones *they* will be.

But with regard to these authors, we have some idea of the early returns. Judging from the sales in the millions and the international reputation and the fact that they are still going strong many decades into it, we are looking at a phenomenon with some clear staying power. That is not the election itself, but it seems like significant results from the exit polls.

Future readers, a century or two out, might make the mistake of calling the twentieth century a truly Christian literary age, because the only writers from that century still being read are overwhelmingly Christian. "Ah," they will say—"a golden age of the Christian faith, when giants walked the earth. Not like today . . ." They will know nothing of all the schlock our age produced.

When it comes to the faith commitments of these writers, there is a general but not universal consensus. We have the Anglicans—Eliot, Lewis, and Capon (Episcopalian). Wodehouse was nominally Anglican and wrote a lot about curates, so we will gladly include him there. There is one Anglican who became Roman Catholic (Chesterton), and one Roman Catholic whose mother had converted from Anglicanism (Tolkien). Mencken was an atheist. Robinson is a Congregationalist, and Nate Wilson is Presbyterian. But as we will see, there is more going on than simply that. Regardless of such details, these are all writers to read.

1

G. K. Chesterton

A WRITER'S LIFE

G. K. Chesterton was baptized as an infant in the Church of England in 1874. He died sixty-two years later, in 1936. Quite a number of wonderful books were produced in the interval.

Chesterton is usually thought of as a Victorian figure, which is certainly when he came of age—Queen Victoria died in 1901, when Chesterton was twenty-seven years old. At the same time, most of Chesterton's real contributions were in the twentieth century. His debates with men like George Bernard Shaw are justly famous, but he also debated men more closely associated with the post-Victorian era, men like Bertrand Russell.

In *Surprised by Joy* C. S. Lewis mentions the impact Chesterton had on his own return to the faith through the book *Everlasting Man*. But he usually speaks of Chesterton as though he was from another era, even though their lives overlapped considerably. Lewis was thirty-eight when Chesterton died, and he was brought back to the faith five years before Chesterton died. And *The Pilgrim's Regress*, Lewis's first Christian book, was published three years before Chesterton died.

Generations overlap, and though I find no indication that Chesterton and Lewis ever met, maybe they walked past each other in a train station once. Someone should write a one-act stage play about that. There certainly was a meeting of the minds between the two and—I would argue—a passing of the baton. Lewis had numerous books by Chesterton in his library, all marked up. The intellectual legacy that Chesterton established was well kept and well tended by Lewis.

As mentioned earlier, Chesterton's parents had him baptized in the established Anglican church, but they themselves tended toward Unitarianism. Chesterton attended the Slade School of Fine Art and took classes in both art and literature. But true to type, he did not finish his degree. Given the times and the way things were, Chesterton spent some time slumming around in free thought before he returned to the Christian faith.

His description of this in *Orthodoxy* is quite amusing. He developed his own philosophy from scratch, and when he was done, he discovered that it was orthodoxy. It was like a great explorer sailing the briny deep in order to discover a new land, and when he had found one, he planted the flag on the beach, and he discovered that his newfound land was a place full of Englishmen.

Chesterton married Frances Bogg in 1901. He was wildly, desperately in love with her, and he stayed that way throughout all their years together. Their chief sorrow was their inability to have children, which was particularly difficult as they both loved children. The closeness of their relationship might seem to be belied by Frances's absence from his autobiography, but she is missing there at *her* request. Perhaps she knew that if he were allowed to write about her at all, he would write about nothing else.

He was sympathetic to the Roman communion through his many years in the Church of England and was eventually brought into the Roman Catholic Church in 1922. He took that step apart from Frances, who stayed in the Anglican communion a few years before she eventually joined him there.

Chesterton made his living as a writer, and it was the lash of journalism that made him write for deadlines. He was a scattered genius, pieces of him everywhere. He once telegraphed his wife,

"Am in Market Harborough. Where ought I to be?" But I think that it can be fairly said that his absentmindedness was due to his great presence of mind. He was all in.

He was a jolly contrarian though not at all irascible. But nevertheless he found himself, again and again, standing against the popular tide. Sometimes it involved literary taste, like his appreciation of Dickens after Dickens had gone out of style. People can be forgiven their foibles and quirks on literary appreciation. But Chesterton also had the ability to oppose the establishment on things that mattered a great deal, as with his opposition to the Boer War, or his valiant opposition to eugenics, or his economic views (called "distributism").

Standing at six feet four inches and weighing almost 290 pounds, Chesterton was renowned for his size. P. G. Wodehouse, in one of his epic expressions, once referred to a large noise as when G. K. Chesterton falls on a sheet of tin.

He was a big man in every sense of the word.

DIGGING DEEPER

Chesterton once said that a paradox is truth standing on its head to get attention. He was a master of paradox in this sense, having an adept way of turning everything upside down so that we might be able to see it right-side up. Chesterton's great gift is that of *seeing*, and being able to get others to *see* it the same way also. In a world gone mad, a dose of bracing sanity is just what many of God's children need to get them through yet another round of the evening news. He bends what is bent so that we may see it straight.

When Chesterton writes about anything, each thought is like a living cell, containing all the DNA that could, if called upon, reproduce the rest of the body. Everything is somehow contained in anything. This is why you can be reading Chesterton on Dickens and learn something crucial about marriage, or streetlights, or something else.

The world is not made up of disparate parts; the world is an integrated whole. God sees it all together and united. When *men* see glimpses of it as all together and united, we say they are prophetic. We call them seers and poets. Chesterton was this kind of man. Not one of us can see it all, but a handful have been gifted to act as though the "all" is actually present there.

It is tempting to call this kind of thing a "worldview," but that seems too structured and tidy somehow. It smells of the classroom, of the right answers checked on a multiple-choice test. A worldview is a good thing, but it is too narrow a word to describe what is happening with Chesterton. When worldview thinking came into vogue in evangelical circles a few decades ago, it has to be admitted that this was a lot better than what had come before that, which was the odd juxtaposition of various inconsistent ideas rattling around in a multitude of Christian heads. Worldview thinking is better than jumbled thinking, but worldview thinking is not the high-water mark.

> In church history, occasionally, like a blue comet on holiday with no schedule to keep, a lonely figure will appear who appears to function fluidly in all three realms [those of prophet, priest, and king], making it look easy. Chesterton was like that. Worldview thinking radiated from him like heat from a stove. This is what systematic thinking should look like, but it hardly ever does.[1]

The problem is not with the word *worldview*. The problem is with what we naturally tend to think of as our eyes. Of course, blindness is not a worldview, and it is an improvement if we move from that blindness to coherent thoughts that we think. A brainview is better than blindness. But the real organ that we must view the world with is the imagination.

Imagination, as Napoleon once remarked, rules the world. One of our great problems is that we have relegated imagination to various artsy ghettos, there to let it play. But imagination, including—especially including—artistic imagination, has to be understood as a practical science. It must govern everything, and if it is detached from the praxis of life and then uprooted, it goes off to the art museums to die.

For Chesterton, an indispensable aspect of the divine imagination is the inclusion of fun. Play, laughter, joy, and mirth are necessary not only for good art but for human well being in all its dimensions. G. K. once said that "in anything that does cover the whole of your life—in your philosophy and your religion—you must have mirth. If you do not have mirth you will certainly have madness."[2]

One of the reasons why Chesterton is such an encouragement to us is that he understands the role of imagination. This is not the same thing as comprehending imagination itself, for no man gets that, but Chesterton does understand the important role that imagination must play. He truly *gets* it, and he practices what he understands.

So when Napoleon said that imagination rules the world—a great aphorism if ever there was one—he was simply giving us some material to work with. In what sense might this be true? In what sense might we get all tangled up in what we falsely think of as imagination?

We should see a distinction between the throne of imagination—the human heart and mind—and the realm of imagination—made up of everything else. One of the central reasons we are languishing in our public life is that we have allowed a divorce between the throne and the realm. Artists are assumed to be the custodians of the imagination, but because of their insistence upon autonomy, they have become like a mad king who has the run of the throne room and nothing else. And out in the mundane realm of ho-hummery, imagination is assumed to be irrelevant.

What this means—when Christians finally wake up to the real state of affairs—is that we are actually besieging a city with no walls and no defenses. If imagination rules the world, perhaps we should focus on getting ourselves some.

Chesterton is famous for paradox, as noted above, but this is an imaginative exercise. Aristotle noted that the use of metaphor was a mark of genius, and I would argue that Chesterton's odd inversions and juxtapositions should be grouped under the broad heading of metaphor.

Chesterton knew that loving and fighting go together. Loving something while being unwilling to fight for it would be better categorized as lust. And at the same time, a man who sees the world in wisdom knows that loving the world means that he must be willing to fight the world. Loving the world means fighting for the world, and loving the world also means fighting the world.

His wisdom made Chesterton a true fighter who rejected the silliness of today's philosophers who want to separate loving and fighting, putting them into separate camps. This attitude is well represented by the glib placard of the sixties, urging us all to make love, not war. This false juxtaposition is trying to hide the fact that it is always both.

Either you make love indiscriminately and make war on the resultant offspring, or you make love to one woman for life and fight to protect her and the children you have fathered. If you determine that it is too militant to fight in the latter way, then the love you have chosen in the former way is simply lust.

We can see that this is how it is unfolding in the West. Lunatic wars and lunatic lusts go together. So do chivalric wars and chivalric romances. The pacifist who doesn't want to fight the dragon for the sake of the lady is actually in the process of becoming a dragon himself. This reality is sometimes obscured by the missing nostril flame and hidden claws, but there is a ready explanation. Pacifists are just passive-aggressive dragons.

Near the end of *Mere Christianity*, C. S. Lewis said this about originality, and it is striking how well it describes Chesterton:

> Even in literature and art, no man who bothers about originality will ever be original: whereas if you simply try to tell the truth (without caring twopence how often it has been told before)

you will, nine times out of ten, become original without ever having noticed it.[3]

Chesterton was a fierce defender of the common man and common things. He defended this so well and ably, and in the way that Lewis describes above, that this made him singularly uncommon. His defense of mundane things was out of this world. His apologetic for the supernatural was the most natural thing in the world.

He once said, speaking of those who like to accommodate themselves to the trends of the times, that "at its worst it consists of many millions of frightened creatures all accommodating themselves to a trend that is not there."[4] It is not that hard to spook a herd. The trend apparently is that things are trending. The buffalos set up a self-authenticating feedback loop, and the plan of action seems obvious to them all and remains such, right over the cliff.

But there are contrarians who don't think matters through any more than the stampeders do, and it doesn't much matter what the fad in question is. It might be iPhones, or N. T. Wright fan clubs, or the election of a welterweight like Obama, or a Taylor Swift concert. Some contrarians are accidentally right when the herd is accidentally wrong, or accidentally wrong when the herd is accidentally right. That's no good either. We need *thoughtful* contrarians—when the house of immovability is built on the foundation of pigheadedness, that house is filled with endless quarrels. When the house is built on the foundation of well-spoken conviction, the home is filled with laughter and joy, though storms may rage outside.

In that same place (speaking of those sociologists who wanted to accommodate themselves to the trend of the time), he noted that in any given moment, the trend of the time at its best consists of those who will not accommodate themselves to anything. Athanasius had to stand *contra mundum*, and it is *he* who is the representative man from that era and not the whole world he had to contend against. *Transit gloria mundi*, with the exception of that courageous glory that is willing to stand up against the glory of all the regnant poobahs. Take Chesterton himself: he hated the insufferable self-importance that lusts to dictate to others what they must do in all the ordinary choices of life. He shows us the path we must take if we want to accomplish the crucifixion of all such coercion.

> Pessimism is not in being tired of evil but in being tired of good. Despair does not lie in being weary of suffering, but in being weary of joy. It is when for some reason or other the good things in a society no longer work that the society begins to decline; when its food does not feed, when its cures do not cure, when its blessings refuse to bless.[5]

The writer Rene Girard calls this kind of social condition a time of sacrificial crisis. Nothing coheres, nothing *tastes*. One of the reasons societies in this state (as we very much are) start to disintegrate is that while drumbeat demands for deeper and greater sacrifice come more rapidly and are insistently louder, the law of diminishing returns has kicked in. It doesn't work anymore.

Generally the resultant hue and cry that sets up calling for shared sacrifice or increased sacrifice or deeper sacrifice is a cry that is lifted up by someone clever enough to want to get out in front of the mob. When crowds are calling for sacrifice, you can depend upon it: they are looking for the sacrifice of somebody *else*. Get in the right position early, man.

This is why, for Christians, all coercion is such a big deal. Simple coercion, absent direct instruction from Scripture, is a big sin; and manipulative coercion, absent clear instruction from Scripture, is also a big sin. The way of vicarious substitution, what Jesus did on the cross, is how he overthrew the coercive principalities and powers. That way of ungodly coercion is doomed forever, and the sooner Christians learn to be done with it, the better.

But the carnal heart turns naturally to making other people do things. This is why we must see the levy, or the referendum, or the law, or the conscription, or whatever it is, and follow it all the way out to the end of the process. When you don't do what they say, men with guns show up at your house. Now this is quite proper when it is the house of a murderer or a rapist or an IRS man from Cincinnati. But suppose it is just a regular guy trying to make a living who had a duck land in a puddle enough times for his land to be declared a wetland? They still show up with guns.

This conclusion has to be developed more, but this is why the substitutionary atonement of Jesus Christ is so important. If Christ died in our place, then this central fact of human history is sheer gift. If we follow the folly of Abelard and say that the death of Christ was mere example, what we have is a way of the cross with no power of grace. And when grace is not center stage, coercion is always standing in the wings.

This is not to deny that Christ died as an example—the apostle Peter absolutely affirms this. But I said *mere* example. Do you see? If Christ died as a substitute, *that* is our example to follow. If he did not, then it isn't. This is why Paul tells husbands to love their wives as Christ loved the church and gave himself up for her (Eph. 5:25). Without this glorious principle of substitution, the way of the cross turns into scolding and hectoring people, and the end of the story is always men with guns. But we should want the men who come to your door to be men with good news of a staggering substitution with lives that match.

How does this relate to Chesterton? On any number of issues, Chesterton was a voice in the wilderness. He stood against the popular coercions. One good example is his opposition to the Boer War in South Africa. Another good example is his stand against those who were bringing in the new "gospel" of eugenics. The Second World War and the Nazi outrages have subsequently made the idea of eugenics a pariah, but we have to understand that before the war, all the cool kids were arguing for "scientific" eugenics. But Chesterton was appropriately dismissive. He said in his book *Eugenics and Other Evils* that he was willing to pay the scientist for what the scientist knew, but that he drew the line at paying scientists for what they didn't know. "Chesterton was particularly concerned with eugenicists' use of state power to achieve their goals."[6] Chesterton was the archetypal underdog, standing up for underdogs.

Modern man, progressive man, has an insatiable lust to interfere with the ordinary things. He strives to become superman and only succeeds in erasing ordinary men. Superman aspirants only become submen. But Chesterton was delighted with common men, the men who work with their hands, have a pint at a pub on the way, and then go home to the wife. What could be more extraordinary?

Not only is this extraordinary; it is also biblical. Those who exalt themselves are humbled, and those who humble themselves are exalted (Matt. 23:12). Chesterton loved to lift up the humble, and he delighted to apply the deft pinprick to those who are puffed up enough that they have begun to float over our heads.

Chesterton could readily speak with inversions because he *was* an inversion. He saw ordinary men as extraordinary, and he was their champion. Extraordinary men, the ones with the bulging foreheads, had plans and schemes and organization and social engineering, and every project they touched became a ruin, uninhabitable by human beings.

The issues that confront us today are just the same as they were in the time of Chesterton, only now they are in front of us in much starker relief. The reason we have trouble seeing them—as Chesterton would have noted for us—is that they are out in plain sight. The more his prophecies are fulfilled, the more difficulty we have in seeing that it is so.

We have gotten to that stage in the battle where the forces have fully joined, and there is no longer—properly speaking—a front. We do not have a distinguishable line anymore. It is more like a melee, with different-colored uniforms everywhere. And this is why every topic has been swept up into the conflict.

Where can you go where the ruling elites will agree to leave you alone? Can you change a lightbulb? Can you fry up some bacon? Can you decline joining in the mandatory celebrations of a same-sex mirage? Can you keep your doctor? Are you allowed to use plastic bags?

Chesterton said in *Orthodoxy* that our task is to fly the flag of the world—and we should know that this is something certain to bring us into conflict with the world. We affirm a fundamental creational loyalty to the world and constantly thwart the world's desire to become disloyal to itself. This is why it is good to be earthy and bad to be worldly. Worldliness is just a clever way of deserting the world. This is the explanation of why worldliness is so consistently weary of the world.

And this is also why a battle in a philosophy class over the correspondence view of truth is connected to the marriage debates, which in turn is connected to the environment, which in turn is connected to just-war theory, which in turn is connected to the correspondence view of truth.

Everything is connected. Everything matters. Nonsense tolerated anywhere will metastasize, and the results are always ugly. "When the people have got used to unreason they can no longer be startled at injustice."[7]

In the broken-windows theory of law enforcement, disregard of the law in petty things signals an unwillingness to deal with *anything*, and so the situation rapidly deteriorates. Some broken windows tolerated will lead to many more broken windows, and it just gets worse from there.

It is the same thing with nonsense. When we refuse to police the boundaries between sense and nonsense in our daily affairs, it is not long before that boundary is ignored everywhere. The death of common sense in ordinary affairs signals the death of common decency everywhere. If you cannot run with men, how can you run with horses (Jer. 12:5)? If you are unwilling to make the right call when it comes to a trifle, what makes you think you will be able to make the right call when the stakes are genuinely high?

This is just one more instance of the centrality of peripherals. And by "centrality of peripherals" I do not mean to veer into my own weird form of zen Presbyterianism—my variation on Chesterton's zen Romanism. This does not mean favoring the peripherals instead of the center. That would be the sin of majoring on minors, swallowing camels, and all the rest of it. But remember, the fruit—which Christ required for identifying the nature of a tree—is way out on the edges of the tree and is at the farthest point away from the root. We must recover the understanding that peripherals are central because the center is important. The root is the most important, and is central, and we test what is central by tasting what is at the edges.

This is one of the reasons why Chesterton is so good at discussing the ordinary issues of life. He can pluck any fruit from any branch and, without changing the subject, trace the life of that fruit back to the root. Take manners, for example. Manners can be described as love in trifles, love at the periphery. The collapse of manners in our society—a peripheral thing, surely!—represents a true downgrade. But here is Chesterton: "Love of humanity is the commonest and most natural of the feelings of a fresh nature, and almost everyone has felt it alight capriciously upon him when looking at a crowded park or on a room full of dancers."[8] Those activities are out at the edges, but by looking at the edges we can see the center.

You give the last piece of pie to God, who doesn't eat pie, by giving it to your neighbor, who does. That is the point of courtesy, manners, and etiquette (consider Rom. 12:10; 13:7; Eph. 6:2; 1 Tim. 5:17; 6:1; 1 Pet. 2:17; 3:7).

The same thing is true in the realm of aesthetics. Relativism has compromised us here as nowhere else. A clearheaded man will want to say that some music, paintings, sculpture, etc., are just plain dumb and stupid. But we immediately hear the retort, "Who is to say . . . ?" Our inability to identify rotten fruit on the branches means that we are especially unable to identify a problem at the root.

There must always be a rich moral soil for any great aesthetic growth. The principle of art for art's sake is a very good principle if it means that there is a vital distinction between the earth and the tree that has its root in the earth; but it is a very bad principle if it means that the tree could grow just as well with its roots in the air.[9]

Some men are prodigies of learning—take Newton, for example, or Pascal—and their towering intellect is about all we can see. Their intelligence is overwhelming. But other men are prodigies of learning, and the more you learn from them, the more ordinary they seem. Chesterton is in this latter category. He is not a man even capable of putting on airs, and yet it seems to me that he could come back to us in our generation almost a hundred years after his death and pick up the conversation right where he left off.

How is this possible? Fads and fashions change, but the permanent things do not change—and Chesterton had through long practice learned to distinguish these things at a glance. The Christian faith is permanently sane and is therefore always a bit out of fashion. Fads and fashions are mild insanities, Chesterton taught, and that is why the church always seems behind the times. It is actually *beyond* the times.

Chesterton has a kind of knowledge that knows what it ought to know, knows what it cannot know, and knows how to delight in the difference:

> A turkey is more occult and awful than all the angels and archangels. In so far as God has partly revealed to us an angelic world, he has partly told us what an angel means. But God has never told us what a turkey means. And if you go and stare at a live turkey for an hour or two, you will find by the end of it that the enigma has rather increased than diminished.[10]

If you have been taught by Chesterton, you will come to see that every unexpected wonder in your life should have been expected. The expected and ordinary things are treasured up as marvels, and you see how they are actually the key to everything. "If you can prove your philosophy from pigs and umbrellas, you have proved that it is a serious philosophy."[11]

So far from it being irreverent to use silly metaphors on serious questions, it is one's duty to use silly metaphors on serious questions. It is the test of one's seriousness. It is the test of a responsible religion or theory whether it can take examples from pots and pans and boots and butter-tubs.[12]

Chesterton knows serious thought takes the world as it actually is. This is quite different from taking it as "serious" thinkers do, locked up as they are in the back recesses of their brainy parts. Taking things seriously in the wrong way is simply a roundabout way of taking yourself seriously, which is actually, come to think of it, the root of all our troubles.

Chesterton was the kind of man who would never take himself seriously, but his lightness about things had nothing to do with the spirit of flippancy. His arguments had weight, and his spirit made them soar. We credit the Wright brothers with inventing an airplane, something that was heavier than air, that could fly. But Chesterton did something very similar first. All his arguments were weighty—heavier than air—and he could make them do hammerheads in the sky.

IF YOU READ NOTHING ELSE

If you are an average reader, you will soon realize that you will not be able to read everything Chesterton wrote. He was prolific in ways that stagger the imagination. Not only was he a prodigy of output, but he was simultaneously a prodigy of scattered disorganization. One hesitates to wonder what he could have done if he had only been organized. What would have happened if he'd had a top-of-the-line laptop and an assistant from tech support to keep explaining it to him? But we hesitate with this thought experiment because we know that if he were here, he would tell us that if he were organized in the ways we propose, he wouldn't have had anything to say. So following is the short list.

When it comes to his writing about the faith, I would recommend *Orthodoxy* and *Everlasting Man*. In the related fields of cultural analysis and engagement, I would also recommend *Brave New Family* and *What's Wrong With the World?*

With regard to his fiction, you should pick up *The Man Who Was Thursday* and some of his Father Brown stories. In terms of structural discipline, his fiction sometimes slouches in the saddle a bit, but it is still engaging and worthwhile.

His collected poems are very worthwhile, and his epic account of King Alfred's heroism, *The Ballad of the White Horse*, should be on your required reading list.

2

H. L. Mencken

A WRITER'S LIFE

With the exception of his five years of marriage, Mencken lived in the same house in Baltimore from his birth to his death, from 1880 to 1956. He once refused a job in New York because it involved leaving his mother. His biographer Terry Teachout describes him as a possible candidate for "mama's boy,"[1] which would conflict mightily with the reputation he had. But it would probably be closer to the truth to describe him as a homebody. He had a lifelong love affair with Baltimore. He was a man of deep attachments and loyalties.

Henry Louis (H. L.) Mencken was quintessentially an American writer, and his loyalties are apparent here as well, although perhaps expressed in a backhanded way. "No other country houses so many gorgeous frauds and imbeciles as the United States, and in consequence no other country is so amusing. Thus my patriotism is impeccable, though perhaps not orthodox. I love my country as a small boy loves the circus."[2]

When he was fourteen, he was seduced by the daughter of a neighbor, and after this, in a different but related realm, he was seduced by T. H. Huxley, the famous agnostic. Huxley was the one who coined the word *agnostic*. That word is composed of the *a* of negation and the Greek word for knowledge, which is *gnosis*. It might be more informative if we used the Latin way of saying it, which would be *ignoramus*. Whatever we might call it, the cloak of "not knowing" allows a considerable license. While Mencken was not as randy as some of his acquaintances, he did want a worldview that offered him scope for what he wanted to do. He was "an occasional visitor to Baltimore's cathouses," and "he conducted various amours with women of more respectable standing."[3]

At the same time, one might sometimes be tempted to think of him as a "reverse hypocrite," someone pretending to be worse than he actually was.[4] The striking (apparent) exception to this sense of loyalty was his manifest relief upon the death of his father, along with an attendant guilt over that relief. But regardless, the Monday after his father's funeral, he presented himself for work at one of the local newspapers.

Prior to his father's death, he had been going to Baltimore Polytechnic, which is truly an odd place for one of America's premier writers to have gained his education. He worked in the family tobacco firm for three years until his father's death, whereupon he bolted. His real education, and the shape of his future career, came from the books he read as a boy, beginning with *Adventures of Huckleberry Finn*. That book had a stupendous impact on him, and we can see in Twain a clear influence on Mencken's voice—they are both distinctively American writers, and both had a deep cynical take on human nature.

From 1899 to 1906, Mencken as writer took off like a rocket—in the Baltimore news business anyway. He rapidly became a big frog in what he was already seeing as a small pond. While his success was gratifying, on that local level he was really only competing with literate drunks and has-beens. Given his work in the world of newspaper writing, it should be obvious that he wrote a lot of editorials and reviews. Influenced by Twain and Ambrose Bierce, Mencken gave up on poetry and fiction and found his distinctive voice in nonfiction commentary, which was definitely his *métier*. Although he gave up on poetry as a vocation, he knew that it was foundational to solid prose writing. A "sense of poetry" is at the bottom of all sound prose. He was ambitious, but given the business he was in, he did not have to move anywhere else in order to pursue that ambition.[5]

Mencken was an *autodidact*, a word that I confess I learned all by myself. As a self-taught man, there were necessarily holes in his education, and this sometimes shows. At the same time, Mencken exhibited the trait that many successful critics tend to display—often wrong, but never in doubt. When he began working on *The Smart Set*, a literary magazine, he became nationally influential as a critic—that is, as an arbiter of taste on a national level. What is the authority of the critic, exactly? Where does it come from? A certain measure of it has to be the capacity to generate fear, which is probably why successful critics generally know how to slash as they write.

He was a writing athlete. And this means that this short biographical sketch has to consist of pointing out the activities of someone who spent years pounding away at a typewriter. For someone who was called upon to crank it out, Mencken certainly went the right direction. In this position, many writers become drudges rather than wordsmithing athletes. It is here that Mencken's vigor is frankly astonishing. He combined the "traditional rigor of British English with the flexibility of the American vulgate."[6] This requires input, and there was a time when he was reading a novel a day (but, of course, most of them had to be dreadful), and he carried a book with him always.[7]

He was with the *American Mercury*, another magazine, between 1924 and 1928. He was married around this time and spent a very pleasant five years as a married man. Mencken had to go through a good bit of mockery for marrying, as his misogynistic fuming in print was well known. Perhaps he was forgiven because he was generally a misanthrope and not just a misogynist. Man, according to Mencken, was the yokel par excellence. He was the booby unparalleled.

Mencken's wife, Sara Haardt, was a professor of English at

Goucher College in Baltimore. They met in 1923 and married after a seven-year courtship. It was a happy union, and when she died of meningitis in 1935, Mencken was grief-stricken.

During the years of the New Deal, he was definitely a cranky outsider. This was a transition time for him. He had been the darling of the outsiders, attacking the old order. But when those outsiders became the new insiders, propping up the fraud that was FDR, Mencken continued to treat the pronouncements of the (new) establishment as just so much more *buncombe*, to use one of his words. Meet the new boss, same as the old boss. His popularity as a writer therefore waned somewhat later in his life, but he was always read, and while his influence had declined, it was still an influence that had not died out entirely.

After a stroke in 1948 he was incapacitated as a writer and ended his last few years as a homebody.

DIGGING DEEPER

C. S. Lewis says somewhere, and I think it is somewhere in the recesses of *English Literature in the Sixteenth Century*, that the color and zest of Elizabethan English is dead and deep. He then says that this gift, long departed from the British Isles, has been inherited by "our American cousins." I think this observation is quite right; in its assorted heyday, American English is full-tilt Elizabethan and all without an Elizabeth for the inspiration. And when I think of this truth, the person who comes to mind immediately is H. L. Mencken.

Few writers have as distinctive a voice as Mencken. Mencken understood that once a natural voice is found, the timbre of that voice should be cultivated, not suppressed. Good writing can "never be impersonal."[8] If you read a detailed account of his life, you will see that Mencken was capable of being a cad. But he was a kindly cad, all things considered. One friend of his said, "I have never known a public figure who was so different from his reputation."[9]

G. K. Chesterton once offered this about Mencken:

I have so warm an admiration for Mr. Mencken as the critic of puritan pride and stupidity that I regret that he should thus try to make himself out a back number out of mere irreligious irritation.[10]

Chesterton allowed that Mencken had been an effective hammer of false idealism and so did not mind that sometimes the hammer was flourished a bit too ostentatiously. But Mencken is so consistently good that it is not surprising that when he misses, it is by way of excess.

Given Mencken's reputation—which anyone who has read *any* quotes attributed to him should know about—it might be surprising to find that "digging deeper" will turn up a thick seam of kindliness. The besetting temptation for every skeptic or cynic (particularly if his gifts for seeing the incongruous are strong) is to become savage or bitter. Sometimes it is hard to tell unless you are there in person, but a good example of the latter would seem to be Frank Zappa's definition of rock journalism, which runs along the lines of people who can't write, interviewing people who can't talk, for people who can't read.

But Mencken was surprisingly not bitter. This was obviously a matter of common grace, since he was such a die-hard unbeliever, but affection actually oozes out of Mencken at every pore. He makes light of things that he really likes—indeed, deeply loves. Here is his evaluation of his parents' marriage and his own upbringing:

> My mother, like any normal woman, formulated a large programme of desirable improvements in him, and not infrequently labored it at the family hearth, but on the whole their marriage, which had been a love match, was a marked and durable success, and neither of them ever neglected for an instant their duties to their children. We were encapsulated in affection, and kept fat, saucy and contented.[11]

We see the same thing in his gratitude. Ironically, this gratitude was suspended "miraculously" on an invisible Kantian skyhook. It is astonishing how grateful he obviously is to no one in particular. His statement that he would choose everything all over again is remarkable.

> And when I mount the gallows at last I may well say with the Psalmist (putting it, of course, into the prudent past tense): The lines have fallen unto me in pleasant places.[12]

One of the most obvious things about his autobiographical *Happy Days* is that Mencken writes in such a way as to make anything an object of fascination. Whether it is soles of shoes that are like slabs of oak, or his own matronly figure, or hired girls built like airplane carriers, or an archbishop collared by Satan, Mencken is consistently, thoroughly interesting. Many Christians, under the influence of pietism, have come to believe that love, affection, and gratitude must always be expressed in such smarmy ways as to ensure its thundering dullness. But in the hands of a gifted writer, the most astonishing connections can be made between *this* and *that*.

In fiction, as we see in Wodehouse, to describe a policeman's shoes as a couple of violin cases slapping up the driveway helps to create an environment of farce. But in nonfictional description, the effect of the same kind of thing is not that of farce; it identifies the author far more than it describes the situation. This is why we must return to the fundamental duty of affectionate loyalty. Mencken was a virtuoso at this kind of thing:

> The liberation of the human mind has been best furthered by gay fellows who heaved dead cats into sanctuaries and then went roistering down the highways of the world, proving to all men that doubt, after all, was safe—that the god in the sanctuary was a fraud. One horse-laugh is worth ten thousand syllogisms.[13]

Returning to a question raised earlier, when it comes to literary criticism, how is it that some people get themselves an audience? What is it that lends the necessary gravitas to the one who would take us all by the hand in order to show us all how the world works, and in particular how the aesthetic world works? Whatever it is, Mencken had it, and we might all profit greatly by discussing this for a moment.

A writer has two basic ways to pull this off. For those who have studied rhetoric, this goes all the way back to Aristotle. The two considerations here are *situated ethos* and *invented ethos* respectively. When it comes to aesthetic criticism and how we are addressing it here, situated ethos is when a successful novelist in his own right is asked his opinion about another novel. His opinion is respected because of who he is known to be—situated ethos. But the critic has to set up shop by himself and pronounce (for example) on a painting when he himself does not know how to paint. He does this by means of some form of invented ethos; that is, he has to come up with various rhetorical devices for getting people to listen. If he is successful at this over time, then he acquires a reputation as a critic and has therefore grown into situated ethos.

A number of people have essayed to define the critic. Christopher Morley said he is a "gong at a railway crossing clanging loudly and vainly as the train goes by."[14] Kenneth Tynan said he is a "man who knows the way but can't drive the car."[15] And Brendan Behan said he is a "eunuch in the harem."[16] But however fun all this is, I think there is more to it than that. And we need to understand that "something more" if we are to understand Mencken.

The critic need not be secure in order to successfully market his wares. He just has to be less insecure than the artists he is criticizing, which, given the temperament of most cape and beret artists post-Rousseau, is not that hard. Consequently, to be literate and able to sneer is about all that it takes to acquire a following somehow, somewhere. The sneer can draw blood just as much as genuine criticism but not nearly as effectively as genuine criticism does.

Being secure and being less insecure are not the same thing, and yet, depending on how this relates to the stand of the critic, each can bring about very similar results. Those insecure folks receiving the criticism are not usually in a position to make such fine distinctions. But whatever the immediate reaction, these two "stands" do not have the same staying power. H. L. Mencken was nothing if not secure in his own opinions. Security exudes from his every pore. But insecurity that tries to mimic this stance accomplishes nothing except bluster, bravado, and shrillness. Mencken's writing still reads well three-quarters of a century after the fact.

The successful critic is one who knows how to "assume the center." This is something that Christians generally need to learn how to do, which is learning how to engage in cultural criticism. Though we tend to do it often, we don't usually do it well. Our cultural criticism tends to be brittle and shrill rather than proceeding from faith. Living by faith includes our criticism, and, oddly enough, the Latin for "with faith" is *con fides*, that is, confidence.

Christians can learn from Mencken in two ways. The first is by watching what he writes on any subject and imitating it. Those who want to be creative originals from scratch seldom are, and those who slavishly follow the recipe have a different problem, just as debilitating. Those who look carefully at the masters to learn and imitate soon find their own distinctive voice with their own contributions.

The second way to learn is by reading and applying his observations about writers, writing, words, and so on. Mencken was a writer who gave much thought to his writing and who was not slapdash. He was meticulous about what he was doing, and he knew where the pitfalls were. Some sample warnings about where a writer should guard himself carefully, according to Mencken, include when he once cautioned against a herd mentality, saying that New York was a kind of "literary slaughterhouse." He said that writers go in on the hoof, and they come out in cans.

A common temptation is to describe a thing rather than do it. Then when it doesn't work out, the writer doubles down and attempts to describe what he is about in even greater detail. But Mencken said this about this peculiar kind of overengineering: a man who knows what every figure of speech is, out to the tenth decimal place, is unlikely to ever be able to make a decent figure of speech himself. Writing by number is no better than painting by number. A wordsmith should be so handy with his tools that he doesn't have to be consulting the manual all the time. Mencken believed that the material substance of fiction is to be retrieved out of life itself and not out of books. And this relates to the importance of love. First-rate writers are more interested in what they are writing *about* than in the fact that they are writing about it. That is why they are interesting.

Mencken wrote preeminently readable prose, just as Chesterton did. It is striking that both men were journalists, and this meant they both had to write for the lash of the deadline. At the same time, even though they were both journalists, they were both standouts from the journalist herd. How is that? What is journalism? What ought it to be?

As Mencken might put it, real journalism is part of a very necessary revolt against the reign of mush. One of the reasons so many modern journalists write so terribly is the objectivity illusion. Marvin Olasky helpfully outlines a number of journalistic "objectivity" idols. They include "straightforward materialism," "balancing of subjectivities," and "disguised subjectivity."[17] In part, this pretense of objectivity is a function of having made the media into a huge machine. It has become a manufacturing plant for verbal widgets, with different words distinguished from one another by the serial numbers on the bottom. Mencken believed that journalism had been mechanized, standardized, and predictable. As such, there was little room left for *characters*.

But in all its forms, a pretense to objectivity necessarily makes for dull writing. An interesting writer draws attention to something other than "the facts." Writing that seeks, at all costs, to highlight the Gradgrind facts and nothing but the Gradgrind facts results in tables, graphs, charts, and prose that could have been written by anyone or by any committee, for that matter. This is why textbooks are now universally dull, as are academic papers, as are newspaper articles and editorials.

The American naturalist John Burroughs once said, "To treat your facts with imagination is one thing, to imagine your facts is quite another."[18] In the grip of the objectivity paradigm, writers think they are refusing to imagine their own facts—when they are actually refusing to think about the facts with an imaginative mind.

The march of this dullness imperative is relentless. Once the news articles submit to the dull mandate, it is just a matter of time before the op-ed page goes the same route. Mencken believed that American newspapers had improved in their news coverage over against his early days in the business, but he thought the editorial page remained the province of dullards.

In *The Devil's Dictionary*, Ambrose Bierce once defined a *luminary* as one who sheds light upon a subject, as a newspaper editor does by not writing about it. In many ways, and especially in small towns, the trick is to write about something without saying anything in particular about it. The duty of journalism was once thought to be to comfort the afflicted and to afflict the comfortable. But imagine trying to live in a small town where a journalist actually took this duty seriously. How likely is it that such a newspaper would be able to maintain this kind of prophetic stance?

Mencken held that journalism in his day had become the profession of mountebanks and cads. This failure was actually inevitable, for only the church has promises that would enable it to maintain this kind of prophetic stand over time. But the attempt by journalism to perform this function, in my view, was the result of secularists filling the vacuum left by the church. That was a vacuum that the church should never have permitted in the first place. The pulpit should be the source for true conviction of sin, whether the town is large or small.

A biblical worldview should teach us that we should expect reversals. "And he said to them, 'You are those who justify yourselves before men, but God knows your hearts. For what is exalted among men is an abomination in the sight of God'" (Luke 16:15). The basic principle here is that that which men naturally and readily esteem, and esteem highly, is an abomination in the sight of God. This is why I think Mencken was so consistently on target. By God's common grace, he took aim at things that Scripture requires us to consider as targets. But because sentimentalism and pietism and other such viral infections in the church had done their work in the nineteenth century, very few in the church were fulfilling this vital prophetic role. Very well, then. God raised up a Philistine to provoke the covenant people to jealousy.

Mencken had an iconoclastic streak, and it would come out at full blast whenever he encountered cant trying to pass itself off as profundity:

> A metaphysician is one who, when you remark that twice two makes four, demands to know what you mean by twice, what by two, what by makes, and what by four. For asking such questions metaphysicians are supported in oriental luxury in the universities, and respected as educated and intelligent men.[19]

He would do this with secular pretenders, but he would also do it when the person in question was a man of the cloth. He said that he was able to resist temptations generally, except when a Methodist bobbed up in front of them in a white choker. Then, he said, he had to either fall upon him or bust. It would be tempting to dismiss all this as simple bigotry, coming from a man not willing to consider anything worthwhile if it came from a Christian quarter. But this would not be an accurate assessment at all. For example, in Mencken's obituary of J. Gresham Machen, his high respect for Machen is obvious:

> The generality of readers, I suppose, gathered thereby the no-tion that he [Machen] was simply another Fundamentalist on the order of William Jennings Bryan and the simian faithful of Appalachia. But he was actually a man of great learning, and,

what is more, of sharp intelligence. . . . Though I could not yield
to his reasoning I could at least admire, and did greatly admire,
his remarkable clarity and cogency as an apologist, allowing
him his primary assumptions.[20]

And it is here that we have yet another example of what it means
to have "a good testimony." Machen won Mencken's respect for
being a man of conviction, even when those convictions put him at
odds with virtually everybody. Mencken saw in Machen a kindred
soul—and I think he was right.

Machen didn't just *say* that he believed the Bible; he really believed it, and when the Prohibition hysteria was gathering steam
in the name of scriptural hand waving, Machen came in with the
actual teaching of the actual Bible and blew all the hypocritical
pretense away. I sometimes wonder how someone like Mencken
would have responded if there had been more Christians like Machen. What would the testimony have been like if Machen had not
been a one-off?

If you read the entire obituary, you can see that when liberals
position themselves to make an appeal to Christianity's "cultured
despisers," the effect is quite the opposite of what they were plan-
ning. And if we can see this as a failed strategy in the analysis of
Mencken, who was capable of dismissing foolish Christians as just
so many simians, then perhaps we should rethink everything. The
liberal thinks that it is the faith that arouses this contempt, when it
is actually the natural response when the faith is held stupidly and
upside down.

> What caused him to quit the Princeton Theological Seminary
> and found a seminary of his own was his complete inability, as
> a theologian, to square the disingenuous evasions of Modern-
> ism with the fundamentals of Christian doctrine. He saw clearly
> that the only effects that could follow diluting and polluting
> Christianity in the Modernist manner would be its complete
> abandonment and ruin. Either it was true or it was not true. If,
> as he believed, it was true, then there could be no compromise

with persons who sought to whittle away its essential postulates, however respectable their motives. Thus he fell out with the reformers who have been trying, in late years, to convert the Presbyterian Church into a kind of literary and social club, devoted vaguely to good works. Most of the other Protestant churches have gone the same way, but Dr. Machen's attention, as a Presbyterian, was naturally concentrated upon his own connection. His one and only purpose was to hold it [the church] resolutely to what he conceived to be the true faith. When that enterprise met with opposition he fought vigorously, and though he lost in the end and was forced out of Princeton it must be manifest that he marched off to Philadelphia with all the honors of war.[21]

Mencken was the kind of man that the liberals were concerned to impress. But look at how unimpressed he was—the "disingenuous evasions of Modernism" were exactly that. How are we supposed to entice honest men with the baubles of our dishonesty? And when we have turned the church into "a kind of literary and social club, devoted vaguely to good works," what have we gained? In order to accomplish this, we had to drive off troublemakers like Machen, who was disrupting our attempts to impress the liberals. But then we see Machen going to Philadelphia to start a believing seminary and are disconcerted to see Mencken standing off to the side, saluting Machen as he goes. Machen had the courage of his convictions, and he had a brain, and he used both of them in the battle. That is enough to win the respect of anyone whose respect is worth having.

One last feature of Mencken's writing should be noted, and that is how vivid and therefore memorable it is. In a letter to Dreiser, Mencken compared bottling beer to preserving roses in cans. Roses in cans? Above all, Mencken's prose is striking; it arrests. He excels at the unexpected. Like a fishmonger, or any other worthy merchant drawing attention to his wares, the writer's job is to attract notice. What he has said needs in some fashion to stand out.

Mencken does this by means of the metaphor. Of all the writers covered in this volume, Mencken and Wodehouse are the ones who lean most heavily on the direct and striking metaphor. Whenever Mencken is cooking in his kitchen, with all his pots on the full boil, you never know beforehand which spices and ingredients he will throw in the pot. But after he has done it, and you have gotten over your surprise, you find yourself nodding your head and thinking, "That *worked.*"

IF YOU READ NOTHING ELSE

On the list of Mencken books you should read is *A Mencken Chrestomathy*. As the title suggests, this is an anthology of the selections that Mencken himself chose. If you enjoy that kind of anthology, there is also *A Second Mencken Chrestomathy*. Next, I would read his autobiographical trilogy: *Happy Days*; *Heathen Days*; and *Newspaper Days*. These books will enable you to see the twinkle in his eye when you are reading any of his stuff that is particularly cutting. "How little it takes to make life unbearable. . . . A pebble in the shoe, a cockroach in the spaghetti, a woman's laugh."[22] A few other books worth considering are *Prejudices*; *The Vintage Mencken*; and *In Defense of Women*.

If you are interested in the craft of writing, his *My Life as Author and Editor* should be on your list. His scholarly work is on display in his magisterial *The American Language* (which I have not completed, as it is a whacking great big book but from which I learned that Thomas Jefferson was the one who coined the word *belittle*).

3

P. G. Wodehouse

Even though P. G. Wodehouse lived a very long life, a sketch of his life might still prove difficult. He once said, "I never want to see anyone, and I never want to go anywhere or do anything. I just want to write."[1] He lived ninety years and wrote more than ninety books, so a Wodehouse timeline will include long segments of him at the typewriter.

Pelham Grenville Wodehouse was born in 1881 and was known for most of his years as Plum, an abbreviation of Pelham. Say Pelham really fast several times and see what happens. He had an easygoing but shy personality. He generally flourished in relationships with closer friends. Though not a public person, neither was he socially maladroit in small societies. He attended Dulwich College, where he excelled as a student athlete (cricket, rugby, and soccer), and was generally well liked by his peers.

He began his illustrious career as a writer working for the school paper, and he churned out a lot of stuff in those early years. A competent writer from the start, he could nevertheless pinpoint the exact time in his life when his very own private muse woke up and whacked him with enthusiasm on the head. He was part way through one of his early books when he suddenly, mysteriously, found his unmistakable voice and proceeded to write with that voice until his death many decades later. After the winding roads of some pretty predictable schoolboy stories, he hit the straightaway and never looked back.

After a time of paying his dues the way serious writers like to do, he became an enormously successful author in the early part of the twentieth century, spent a good deal of time hopping back and forth between Britain and America, got into scrapes with the IRS, was hired as a screenwriter in Hollywood more than once, was paid a lot there for doing very little, wrote lyrics for Broadway productions, and, most importantly, established himself as the master of the comic short story and novel. His ability to produce hot stuff on demand was uncanny, and in the course of his life he wrote ninety-some novels and innumerable short stories.

Wodehouse was living in France with his wife, Ethel, when the Second World War broke out, but remaining there turns out to have been a mistake. He did not leave for England because he was working on a novel, and because he probably could not have gotten his pet dog (a Pekingese) with him back into England. He was consequently captured and spent some time in a concentration camp for foreign civilians. On the eve of his sixtieth birthday, after he was released by the Germans because of his age, the stage was set for him to create the one great controversy of his life, which was his agreement to do some broadcast talks from Germany to America. Though the radio talks were entirely nonpolitical, recounting his experiences in the concentration camp, and were directed to the United States, which was not yet in the war, the effect in Britain was nonetheless explosive. Despite the fact that the broadcasts were not heard in England, the content of the talks was assumed, and Wodehouse was denounced as a turncoat scoundrel and accused of treason. He thought he was just exhibiting a humorous stiff-upper-lip approach to a difficult situation, but the affair was not driven by his intentions.

Judged by content, the talks were certainly unoffensive, but judged by context, they were damning. Those who knew him understood that he was about as apolitical as a man can get without being an oyster, and, consequently, they understood that he had been more than a little naive about how the Germans would use his talks. But they knew that this was all he had been—naive. When it finally dawned on him how foolish he had been, he was as appalled as anyone, but the damage was already done. He was initially thought by his countrymen to have been a cad and a traitor, when what he really had been was merely a chump.

Because of the controversy, he was unable to return to Britain after the war, so he settled on Long Island, where he stayed for the remainder of his life and was eventually naturalized as an American citizen. The British were very slow to forgive him, but when they finally did, they did it in style, and Queen Elizabeth II knighted him in 1975, two months before he died. He died at home at the age of ninety, still working on another novel. Not many men are able to work fruitfully into their nineties, but Wodehouse produced some of his best work in his latter years. He was certainly not a writer who crested early.

Not surprisingly, many readers of this book are likely interested in his religious commitments. There is never any neutrality, not even at a place like Blandings Castle. His faith is hard to ascertain from the available information, but it is safe to say at least four things about it. First, he was baptized in the Church of England at St. Nicolas' Church in Guildford. His father was a judge in Hong Kong, and his mother was visiting England when Pelham was born prematurely. His connection to the church was predictable, respectable, and staid.

Second, his knowledge of the Bible was pretty thorough (perhaps he had won the same kind of Scripture Knowledge Award that his Bertie Wooster had prized so earnestly). His easy familiarity with Scripture is revealed constantly throughout his books, and he could nail down an allusion as quickly as Jael, the wife of Heber.

Third, the only direct information on his faith I could find was his reference to his attendance on the ministry of a Salvation Army colonel during his time in concentration camp. As he put it, "I got very religious in camp. There was a Salvation Army colonel there who held services every Sunday. There is something about the atmosphere of a camp which does something to you in that way."[2]

And last, for a Christian, the world he portrays has some very familiar lines of latitude and longitude. Wodehouse simply assumes a Christian order, an established church, and a fairly respectable (albeit dull) clergy scandalized by the occasional orangutan in orders. What he never challenges throughout all his books is extremely revealing. His world, admittedly idealized, is one in which Christian readers find themselves very comfortable. Apart from the pinching of policemen's helmets by young curates, blinded as they were by love of one of Wodehouse's antinomian girls, the moral universe he paints is generally a recognizable one. True, there is an occasional stray *hell* or *damn*, and this is unfortunate, because many modern Christians do all their worldview analysis through the simple process of counting them. Nevertheless, taking one thing with another, the world in Wodehouse has to be seen as being right-side up.

The plots in Wodehouse, on the other hand, are farcical and labyrinthine, and it must be admitted that there are not many of them. They basically amount to some poor fish on a slab wanting to pledge his troth to some lovely young pippin, and the bride price he must pay is the task of kyping something valuable while staying at a spacious country manor. The young woman adored is lovely and svelte and has limpid eyes that swim slowly over what she sees. She is also frequently a thug. There are exceptions to and variations on this setup of course, but one gets the basic idea. The farce gets tangled up in aunts, bookies, butlers, fierce secretaries, gentlemen's personal gentlemen, and professional thieves, and by the time all is done, a wonderful time has been had by all. To paraphrase the master at this point, if all the good times available from his books were laid end to end, they could reach part of the way to the north pole.

As a stylist, Wodehouse was, of course, superb, writing balanced and nuanced sentences that, taking the hay with the straw, just wouldn't quit. But the thing that made him a supreme writer, the thing that ensures a readership many years from now, was his genius in working with metaphor, and metaphors that were like metaphors, like similes, if you catch the drift. Whether the thing under discussion was subdued and quiet, like bees fooling about in the flowerbed, or farcical and ludicrous, like the high-octane sappiness of Madeline Bassett, who believed the stars to be God's daisy chain, the metaphors and similes found in the work of Wodehouse cause the reader, even if alone, to laugh like a hyena with a bone caught in its throat. Or perhaps the laughter of some other more genteel readers might more closely approximate the sound of glue being poured from a jug. In *Very Good, Jeeves* we have this immortal description:

> I once got engaged to his daughter Honoria, a ghastly dynamic exhibit who read Nietzsche and had a laugh like waves breaking on a stern and rockbound coast.[3]

But in any case, Wodehouse has the constant capacity to surprise his readers with a sudden turn or twist of phrase, and to surprise them pleasantly.

The effect is not unlike the pleasure received when one thinks one has been disgracing his family through robbing banks and wakes up to discover it was all a dream. And on every page too.

So Wodehouse began writing in the early twentieth century and continued writing down to his death in 1975. He was widely acclaimed as a stylist on both sides of the Atlantic, and not by slouches either. Rudyard Kipling once said that "Lord Emsworth and the Girlfriend" was the best short story in English literature.[4]

DIGGING DEEPER

Machines are serious business, and since modernity likes to run like a machine, modernity is therefore very much like those four attorneys—dour, solemn, somber, and gray. Instead of laughing at this spectacle, many orthodox folks who ought to know better muddle along grimly as best they can. But something really should be done about all this, and part of that "something" needs to include acquiring a familiarity with the Wodehousean canon and a concomitant acquaintance with the importance of modern Dutch cow creamers.

On one level, reading the works of P. G. Wodehouse provides its own justification, provided you are looking to justify the reading of light comedy at the beach. But who actually needs to justify that kind of thing? To consume a literary souffle brings its own reward and no heavy, sick feeling afterward. Tangled plots, no sex or violence, memorable characters, hilarious dialog—what could be better? When I say "no sex," I mean nothing beyond flirting and random engagements to the wrong people mostly. There is *some* sin present, to be sure, but it mostly involves the pinching of cow creamers at English country estates, blackmail of scoundrels, not to mention high levels of deception to get out of difficulties with troublesome aunts.

So Wodehouse really is a fun read. But how could pursuit of Wodehouse ever be a *serious* task? I would suggest that anyone who wants to be a serious writer needs to be thoroughly acquainted with Wodehouse, and for two basic reasons: it is pleasurable, and it is good for you. Anyone who wants to enjoy reading good writers needs to emphasize the first. For those who simply want to learn how to read, this is light reading that is not junk food.

Wodehouse knew how to describe, in painfully accurate ways, the foibles of those who wanted to be serious writers. Reading Wodehouse can help keep you from wanting to be the wrong kind of serious writer, by which I mean a poet who might write something appalling like *The Pale Parabola of Joy*, and who might have allowed himself to be named something like Ralston McTodd. Wodehouse was merciless to pretentiousness, and aspiring writers are the most pretentious fellows on the planet. So there's that spiritual benefit.

But the second reason is why I have for years been devoting myself to an ongoing and consistent reading of Wodehouse—meaning that I am always reading something by him, all the time. Simply put,

Wodehouse is a black-belt metaphor ninja. Evelyn Waugh, himself a great writer, once said that Wodehouse was capable of two or three striking metaphors per page. He looked like a sheep with a secret sorrow. One young man was a great dancer, one who never let his left hip know what his right hip was doing. She had just enough brains to make a jaybird fly crooked. Her face was shining like the seat of a bus driver's trousers. He had the look of one who had drunk the cup of life and found a dead beetle at the bottom.

The metaphors are consistently laugh-out-loud funny, but they are more than that. They are arresting. They are memorable. They connect things that are not usually connected. They show wordsmiths how wordsmithing needs to be done, but they also help ordinary folks liven up the discourse of their lives. Aristotle once said that the ability to use metaphor rightly is a mark of genius, and if this is correct, as I believe it is, then Wodehouse has a lot to teach anyone who deals with words—which would be all of us. We learn by imitation, and when it comes to striking similes and metaphors, Wodehouse is worthy of imitation, though it is difficult to imitate the inimitable. But to imitate, we must read, so exposure to Wodehouse can show us how.

We need to look elsewhere for the *why*. Ultimately, I believe that Christians should love metaphor because we are servants of the Logos, the Word. The Word was *with* God, the Word *was* God, the Word *became* flesh. What we have here is the basic foundation for a theology of metaphor. We have distinction, we have identification, and we have incarnation. What else would anyone dealing with words need?

One of the shared assumptions between modernists and post-modernists is the idea that metaphor is meaningless. The modernists say this, and so they go and look for meaning somewhere else. The liberal arts must be for people who are squishy on truth. The post-modernists agree that metaphor is meaningless but then want to say that everything is metaphor. The modernist wants to find objective truth raw and thinks he must do it by means of science or reason.

He must discover the formula, for that is where meaning has to reside if we are to have certainty. The postmodernist says that such ventures are futile. *Everything* is metaphor, and so nothing can be the carrier of fixed and objective truth.

Both positions have a point—the modernist is right that there is such a thing as objective meaning, and the postmodernist is right that everything is metaphor. But these two inconsistencies can be reconciled in Christ, and only there. Moreover, these two apparent inconsistencies have to be reconciled—intellectual life in an incoherent mess unless we reconcile them.

Because Jesus is the ultimate metaphor of God, Christians can grant that all is metaphor but still say in confidence that this is why everything has meaning. We tend to assume a necessary downgrade of meaning whenever there is motion, whether between word and object, or between the poet Burns's love and a red, red rose. When we move from word to referent, we think we are leaping from crag to crag, across an abyss below. If we slip, we have had it.

But this assumption is itself dependent on a metaphor, as though meaning has to get increasingly smudgy every time we make a xerox copy of it. But suppose it is not like that. What if God has created the world in such a way that meaning gets clearer and crisper each time we move it properly? Suppose information improves in transmission.

Christians worship, serve, and imitate God the writer, God the written, and God the reader, and within the triune Godhead there is no degradation of meaning, even though the communication is infinite. The Logos was *with* God, and the Logos *was* God, and the distinction between them did not introduce any corruption. There is no downgrade of meaning between God the speaker and God the spoken. Neither is there a downgrade of meaning between God the spoken and God the listener. The Word is the *express* image of God the Father (Heb. 1:3), with no falling short and no remainder. God writes, and God is written. Not only so, but God himself reads what is written—he is his own interpreter.

But God hath revealed them unto us by his Spirit: for the Spirit searcheth all things, yea, the deep things of God. (1 Cor. 2:10 KJV)

All of this is to say that when we use a metaphor wisely or appropriately, we are not skidding away from the truth but rather converging on it. We are finite, and so we cannot speak or comprehend the ultimate metaphor all at once, and so we have to layer them. We have to use a multitude of metaphors—and the more we use them fittingly, the more we grasp what God is like. This is why using metaphor a lot can be such a helpful thing. And for those who think we may have wandered from the point, Wodehouse uses metaphor a lot and does so overtly, explicitly.

Everything holds together in Christ, and when two disparate things are brought together in an incongruous and yet brilliant metaphor, we see that this can work only because there is a logical bedrock upon which the entire cosmos is built. We do not live in a house built on sand. Metaphor works for a reason. The walls in this house are straight for a reason. The corners go together and fit for a reason.

Part of the reason it works is that the dissimilarity *arrests*. The universe goes together in some very odd ways. But it doesn't go together *any* old way. It is complicated, layered, structured, and subtle. It is not random. This is why you can have bad metaphors—of the kind you can easily find on the Internet simply by using the search terms "bad metaphors"—the terms of which are right next door to each other, but which don't work, except by being funny in their not working. For example: "He was as tall as a six-foot-three-inch tree." Or this: "John and Mary had never met. They were like two hummingbirds who had also never met."

Compare this to the peerless reach that Wodehouse has: "Some minds are like soup in a poor restaurant—better left unstirred." Or this: "He felt like a man who, chasing rainbows, has had one of them suddenly turn and bite him in the leg."

One plausible counterargument that might be made against the metaphorical value of Wodehouse is that his metaphors are all *comic.* They are outlandish and frequently laugh-out-loud funny, and surely the cosmos is not to be understood as comedy hour. I once heard a friend object that to be steeped in the language of the prophets and to be steeped in Wodehouse were strikingly different matters.

There are several responses to this. The first is that the cosmos *is* a comedy, not in the sitcom sense, obviously, but in the classic sense of ending happily with a wedding—the New Jerusalem descends out of heaven like a bride adorned for her husband. This means that farce and absurdity fit within this framework in a very different way than absurdity fits within a nihilistic framework. In the latter setup, the absurdity *is* the framework. But when we live wisely in the world God put us in, humor works because every straight *line* in the cosmos is also serving as a straight *man*.

The second response is that comic metaphors can still teach us how all metaphors work, how the thing is done. Reading through Wodehouse has any number of moments to make one snort, and reading through Lamentations does not. But this does not mean that *Leave It to Psmith* and Lamentations belong to two different worlds. The tone is different, but it is all God's world. Comic metaphors are kind of "out there," and it is therefore easy to see how they work. Somber metaphors, gray metaphors, and slow-walking metaphors will all work the same way.

> He has besieged and enveloped me
>   with bitterness and tribulation;
> he has made me dwell in darkness
>   like the dead of long ago.
>
> He has walled me about so that I cannot escape;
>   he has made my chains heavy. (Lam. 3:5–7)

We don't have a problem teaching little children to form their letters on paper with wide lines, the kind of paper that still has the bark in it. They learn to do this with comparative ease, and they shape their letters to smaller and more difficult parameters later on. In the same way, because comic metaphors are easier—I think because they are *fun*—we can compare this to that and make ourselves laugh. But when we are done, we still know how to compare this with that.

The simple outlandishness of Wodehouse's metaphors is not what makes them funny. The metaphysical poets—men like Herbert and Donne—use metaphors that are artificial and contrived, but that doesn't make them comic.

In addition, a comic outlook as metaphorical bedrock helps protect us against another common failing. We need Wodehouse for a number of reasons, but one stands out. The besetting sin of many cranky, conservative Christian types is their inability to make any good point whatever without sounding shrill. And the better the point, the shriller the making of it can be. The more serious the point, the shriller it gets. When it gets down to matters of life and death, we sound like so many teakettles on a full boil.

We try to defend ourselves against criticism of this fault by pointing to how serious the whole issue is. But this is a lame defense. If it is all *that* serious, then why do we insist on communicating with others about whatever it is in ways that are lame and self-defeating? If it is so serious, shouldn't we want to communicate in a way that is effective? Why is ineffective screeching the right response to an imposing challenge? Shrillness is therefore a lazy man's indignation. Shrillness is cheap bluster.

If our words are weapons—and they are—then we need to train ourselves in the use of them. It is quite possible that a novice doesn't see the connection between this particular swordplay drill and what he could do in an actual battle, but he doesn't see this because he is the novice. An ability to respond on the spot with a bon mot is winsome. And as D. L. Moody once put it, if you are winsome then you win some.

But in the training for every worthwhile endeavor, it is always possible for the newbies to complain that they don't see the relationship between their boot camp drills and the overall mission. If they could see it, they would already be trained, and it is manifest that they aren't.

So adeptness in metaphor should not be sprinkled on top of the content. Far better to have the "style" woven into the substance of the argument itself. The nineteenth-century preacher John Broadus once put it this way:

> The best style attracts least attention to itself, and none but the critical observer is apt to appreciate its excellence, most men giving credit solely to the matter, and having no idea how much the manner has contributed to attract and impress them.[5]

In *Surprised by Joy*, C. S. Lewis makes a very similar point about Chesterton:

> His humour was of the kind I like best—not "jokes" imbedded in the page like currants in a cake, still less (what I cannot endure), a general tone of flippancy and jocularity, but the humour which is not in any way separable from the argument but is rather (as Aristotle would say) the "bloom" on dialectic itself. The sword glitters not because the swordsman set out to make it glitter but because he is fighting for his life and therefore moving it very quickly.[6]

The point is that style or metaphors are not some kind of add-on extra. They are part of how our minds are shaped. And reading someone whose mind is shaped (or warped, as the case may be) in a particular way is to be shaped in a similar way. "Whoever walks with the wise becomes wise, but the companion of fools will suffer harm" (Prov. 13:20). He who walks with the metaphorical will become metaphorical, so to speak.

My wife and I are blessed with three children, all of whom have grown up into marvelous writers. A rigorous grammatical education was part of the early training for this, but it was fairly soon in their secondary education—as we were reading their papers written for school—that we began to detect the looming presence of

Wodehouse in virtually everything they wrote. And, as it seems to me, this was not a press-wood veneer on particle board but rather a manifestation of the kind of hardwood that had grown over a number of years.

So to have been well marinated in the writing of Wodehouse is to have been soaked in the . . . , well, it is to have been marinated in, you know, his writings. The sunniness of his prose coupled with his robust prowess in the realm of insult are exactly what we need in these, our troubled times. For we are not just doing battle with the powers of darkness; we are also engaged in mortal conflict with the theology of Madeline Bassett, resident theologian and high priestess of pop evangelicalism.

IF YOU READ NOTHING ELSE

For the poor, benighted souls who have not had the pleasure, where is one to begin his recommending? But first, a warning. If someone simply wants to say they have "read Wodehouse," we may note in the first instance that they would only say this because they have not read him. Once they have undertaken the happy chore, the desire to continue is motivated differently than perhaps it began. And about time.

For those who are unacquainted with his work, the size of his pile can be intimidating, and it has to be recognized that while the quality of his books is remarkably and consistently high, there are still some works that stand out, like eager public servants, and that will reward the new student of his *oeuvre*, and reward him quick and hard, usually by the second page. In this age of instant gratification, fast food, fast-lane commuting, and tele-right-nowing, it is wonderful to find great literature that is capable of doing exactly the same thing. Some great lit just competes with other great lit. But it takes extraordinary lit to compete with drivel—and on its own level, too.

For the novels, the place to begin is with *Leave It to Psmith*; *The Code of the Woosters*; *Aunts Aren't Gentlemen*; *The Mating Season*; and *Right Ho, Jeeves*. For the short stories, a good start is the Mulliner stories and the Drones Club stories (both are available in single volumes). Usually this fair start will prove to be an introduction to a lifetime of enjoyment. And if this is somehow inexplicably not the case, then the fact that the books read "on assignment" were among Plum's best reveals exactly where the problem is. It is probably to be found in the fact that the disapproving reader is a complete chump.

So let's suppose I have sold you. As was mentioned already, Wodehouse wrote about ninety books—where should you *start*? Virtually everything he writes is about the same general world, but there are recurring casts of characters within certain subsets of his books—numerous Jeeves books, numerous Blandings Castle books, and so on.

I think you would get a very solid grasp of what you might expect if you were to read four books. The references here are to editions being put out by the Overlook Press, folks who are engaged in the worthy task of rereleasing the entire Wodehouse collection in an affordable hardback collection. The first is, of course, *The Code of the Woosters*. The most famous of all Wodehouse characters, Jeeves and Bertie Wooster, are found here. Another set of memorable characters is found in *Galahad at Blandings*, including the absentminded Lord Emsworth. *Leave It to Psmith* is, in my view, one of his best. The *P* in Psmith is silent. And if you are not very adventurous, and want to stick close to the shore, you might want to start with *Meet Mr. Mulliner*, a representative collection of short stories.

Incidentally, a word should be put in here about the recent series of Jeeves and Wooster pieces done by the BBC and available in video. These are very well done and quite humorous in their own right, but one caution must still be noted. The very best thing about the work of Wodehouse, namely, his powers of description, is necessarily absent. In a video, a constable can certainly be shown walking, but there is no way to picture him doing so with his shoes clumping along like a couple of violin cases.

4

T. S. Eliot

A WRITER'S LIFE

Thomas Howard is exactly right when he notes that T. S. Eliot's poetry "had made him the giant of English poetry in the twentieth century."[1] But his enormous influence on the letters of Western culture began in an out-of-the-way place.

Like Huck Finn, T. S. Eliot was a son of the Mississippi. He was born in St. Louis in 1888 and brought up there. He returned to his family's New England roots when he attended Harvard, and shortly after that he became an American expatriate in England. But toward the end of his life there, he returned again to his New England roots in his poetry.

He came from a Unitarian home, which in my view affected him deeply. His angular severities came from somewhere. His ancestry also affected him—one of his ancestors, Andrew Eliot, who sailed from East Coker (which shows up in *Four Quartets*), was one of the judges in the Salem witch trials.

His education was at Harvard, then at the Sorbonne, and finally at Merton College in Oxford. His early poetry began to be published as soon at 1909, but he really began to gain significant recognition for his poetry in 1917 with the publication of *Prufrock and Other Observations*.

He married Vivien Haigh-Wood in 1915. Their marriage was

troubled from the beginning, and they finally separated in 1933. Vivien had been unstable from the start, and she was eventually confined to an asylum, dying there in 1947.

Eliot also had a long-standing, ambiguous relationship with a woman named Emily Hale. He wrote her about a thousand letters, which are to be opened in the year 2019, the point at which a number of people will say, "Well, now we know." While it is quite possible that we will discover something scandalous in 2019, it is much more likely that we will reaffirm something that is already apparent from the public record: Eliot was a man of intense poetic and religious scruples, and Emily Hale appears to have been Beatrice to his Dante.

T. S. Eliot founded *The Criterion* in 1922, a leading literary journal until its closure in 1939. Eliot received the Nobel Prize in 1948, along with one of England's highest honors, the Order of Merit. In 1958, the Archbishop of Canterbury invited both Eliot and C. S. Lewis to serve on the Commission to Revise the Psalter, which resulted in a surprising friendship. They had not really been chummy before that, largely due to very different visions of what poetry should be and do—it might fairly be said that C. S. Lewis had been one of Eliot's literary adversaries. In fact, there was one episode in 1926 when Lewis and some friends tried to prank Eliot by submitting a send-up of modernist poetry to *The Criterion*. The poem began with "My soul is a windowless façade." If Eliot had published it, there would have been a great deal of hilarity, but he never responded. Lewis was not yet a Christian; that was to happen a few years later.

But his suspicion of Eliot continued into his Christian life. For those familiar with *The Pilgrim's Regress*, Eliot is the figure of Angular in that book. In *Preface to Paradise Lost*, Lewis takes issue with Eliot this way: "If Mr. Eliot disdains the eagles and trumpets of epic poetry because the fashion of this world passes away, I honour him. But if he goes on to draw the conclusion that all poetry should have the penitential qualities of his own best work, I believe he is mistaken. As long as we live in merry middle earth it is necessary to have middle things."[2]

At the same time, Lewis said, "I agree with him about matters of such moment that all literary questions are, in comparison, trivial."[3]

Lewis never could figure out what made Eliot think of a patient etherized on the table when he looked at a sunset. Lewis wrote one poem, entitled *A Confession*, which he began this way:

I am so coarse, the things the poets see
Are obstinately invisible to me.
For twenty years I've stared my level best
To see if evening—any evening—would suggest
A patient etherized upon a table;
In vain. I simply wasn't able.

At the same time, he did have some significant appreciation for Eliot's poetic gift. C. S. Lewis said this: "In reading Mr. Eliot one seems to be listening to a voice that is always on the point of dying away—no poetry can more powerfully convey the sense of stillness, hushed expectancy, vacancy, death."[4]

Eliot had inherited more than a little gnosticism from his Unitarian upbringing, and a good measure of it stayed with him through his conversion. When he had become a leader in the modernist literary school through his poem *The Waste Land* (1922), Eliot was largely misunderstood by his enthusiastic followers. He wrote modern poetry in *form*, but he was a thoroughgoing classicist in his methods, discipline, and education. He was a nonbeliever approaching the point of *fin de siecle* despair, and the crowd went wild. Then, when he took the next appropriate step and became a Christian, no one knew what to do or where to look.

His poems are allusion-soaked, so much so that it is very hard to follow unless you are as well educated as he was, which would be difficult. Unfortunately, the same sensation of a spreading bewilderment can be accomplished by the aspiring ignoramus, and so there we are. But even for the one who doesn't catch the drift of the poems, some of the lines are still spectacular:

- At the still point of the turning world . . .

- The fever sings in mental wires.

- Undisciplined squads of emotion.

- Ash on an old man's sleeve / Is all the ash the burnt roses leave.

- Streets that follow like a tedious argument.

- I should have been a pair of ragged claws / Scuttling across the floors of silent seas.

Eliot was not just significant as a playwright and poet; he also made important contributions as a Christian thinker in his essays. One book currently in print is called *Christianity and Culture*, in which are many important insights that we in particular need to hear. For example, he spoke there of the illusion (still widespread, despite everything) that "there can be culture without religion."[5]

> We may go further and ask whether what we call the culture, and what we call the religion, of a people are not different aspects of the same thing: the culture being, essentially, the incarnation (so to speak) of the religion of a people.[6]

One Reformed writer, Henry Van Til, has observed that culture is religion externalized. Though this insight can be abused, Eliot affirms the core truth in it. Every culture has a religious center, and every religion, like a seed, given water, sunlight, and nutrients, grows up into a particular plant.

> What is wanted is not to restore a vanished, or to revive a vanishing culture under modern conditions which make it impossible, but to grow a contemporary culture from the old roots.[7]

But culture is something that must grow; you cannot build a tree, you can only plant it, and care for it, and wait for it to mature in its due time.[8]

T. S. Eliot died in 1965 and was buried in the parish church, St. Michael, East Coker—the title of one of the four quartets—in Somerset, England.

DIGGING DEEPER

If we want to reflect more deeply on Eliot as a mature poet and thinker, the place to go is *Four Quartets*. The quartets are named, in succession, *Burnt Norton*; *East Coker*; *The Dry Salvages*; and *Little Gidding*. On the view that you can't tell the players without a scorecard, the explanations for these quaint place names will follow in a moment. Let Thomas Howard explain our difficulty: "Readers fret over Eliot's habit of treating us as though we know as much as he did."[9]

Burnt Norton is named after a ruined country house in Gloucestershire, and it is a meditation on time. *East Coker* takes its name from a village in Somerset and was the home of one of Eliot's ancestors, which he left to go to America in the seventeenth century. *The Dry Salvages* is named for a small cluster of rocky islands with a lighthouse off the coast of Massachusetts. *Little Gidding* was the name of an Anglican monastery in the seventeenth century, a place renowned for its devotional life.

Notice that the progress of the poetry here is England, England as a point of departure for America, America, and then back in England—just like the Eliots. Eliot's people had been English; one of them had left East Coker for America; Eliot had grown up in middle America but vacationed in Massachusetts as a boy, went to Harvard there, and then returned to England.

As the entire body of Eliot's work is considered, one reason for focusing on *The Four Quartets* is that this represents his mature Christian outlook. In this earlier work, he very much represented the mind and spirit of the modern (unbelieving) age. Eliot's despair was prelude to his repentance, while the despair of the rest of his lost generation was just causing them to circle the drain.

But even after his conversion, there was room for some debate. In the first Christian book that C. S. Lewis wrote, *The Pilgrim's Regress*, he treats a number of the men and movements of the twentieth century, and it is not surprising that Eliot is one of them.

> Chad Walsh points out that Angular is a caricature of T. S. Eliot. Eliot's well-known Anglo-Catholicism is suggested by Angular's name, but it is Eliot's dry anti-Romantic approach to literature as well as religion that Lewis is satirizing.[10]

It was not for nothing that Lewis pegged Eliot as *Angular*. He lived north of the east/west road in *Regress*, a symbol for severity as Lewis viewed it, as opposed to the swampy sensuality that was located south of the road. Lewis was identifying Eliot as an ascetic. That was in fact his natural disposition, and it was a disposition that remained after he became a Christian. He was a stringent man. But even though he rejected what he would think of as the gaudiness of romanticism, he was nevertheless fully capable of producing poetry of great beauty. And in the minds of some, "great beauty" would be an understatement.

> *Four Quartets* stands as Eliot's valedictory to the modern world. I myself would place it, along with Chartes Cathedral, the *Divine Comedy*, van Eyck's "Adoration of the Mystic Lamb," and the Mozart Requiem, as a major edifice in the history of the Christian West.[11]

Nothing like a little pressure when all you were doing was trying to write a poem.

Thomas Howard, the Roman Catholic writer cited above, argues that Eliot was capable of writing such superb verse because he was a Christian and a sacramentalist. He seeks to account for Eliot's poetic scope this way:

But Eliot, being a Christian and a sacramentalist, believes that the physical is the very mode under which we make our way along to our destiny (*telos*) and that the effort to shuffle off the physical, or to deplore it, is both misbegotten and disastrous.[12]

Howard also adds this:

This outlook is characteristic of Roman Catholicism, Anglicanism, and Orthodoxy: Protestantism tends toward the disembodied, focusing rather on the great abstractions of divine sovereignty, grace, atonement, justification, and worship that shun as much as possible the physical.[13]

I don't want to say that this point has absolutely *nothing* to it, but I think we must say—and the character of Eliot requires us to say—that it just ain't that simple. Eliot was a fastidious man and with an ascetic turn of mind. *The Four Quartets* is great poetry, but it is great poetry by someone who is not exactly *comfortable* with earthy things just the way they are. And the much maligned Puritans were the ones who had actually reintroduced earthiness into lives of complete devotion—not to mention into their poetry.

Again, we find C. S. Lewis on the opposite side. He put it this way:

There is no understanding the period of the Reformation in England until we have grasped the fact that the quarrel between the Puritans and the Papists was not primarily a quarrel between rigorism and indulgence, and that, in so far as it was, the rigorism was on the Roman side. On many questions, and specially in their view of the marriage bed, the Puritans were the indulgent party; if we may without disrespect so use the name of a great Roman Catholic, a great writer, and a great man, they were much more Chestertonian than their adversaries.[14]

Lewis uses the phrase "indulgent party," but in this discussion we might call them the *earthy* party. Leland Ryken has a fine book on the Puritans that aptly calls them *The Worldly Saints*. We are victims of anachronistic slander if we think that the Puritans were in any way, well, puritanical. *That* term came to be applied to the bluenoses and wowsers well after the Puritan party had brought back into Christian discipleship an incarnational embrace of all material things. The earth is the Lord's, and the fullness thereof.

So if we say that Eliot was a great poet because he was *not* a Puritan, then how can we explain Milton, who was one? If we say Eliot had an inside track because he was a sacramentalist, then what do we do with Marvell, who wasn't one? We want to be careful that we don't participate in an unseemly scramble for the big names to adorn our position, as though theology were a particular kind of shaving cream that needs a second baseman for the Yankees to endorse it.

But at the same time, it should be intuitively obvious that one's theology of the Word has some kind of relevance to the use of words. And it should also be obvious that different branches of Christendom will, with their varying emphases, find themselves creating different effects. The point that Howard makes about Eliot could be made, I think with much greater justice, about Gerard Manley Hopkins, who was a sacramentalist and, in his appreciation of earthbound things, almost a Puritan.

And as there are theological differences, so there will be divisions over the cultural impact it will all make. As a Reformed minister, I am obviously much more sympathetic to the claim that the Reformation made a constructive difference in the realm of aesthetics than Thomas Howard would be. That is to be expected.

> From this perspective the Reformation can be seen as an infinitely varied, but coherent and extended, metaphor for the bountifulness of God's grace. If, however, there is anything to be said for this argument, then we are going to have to look in quite a new way at Protestantism, which—we have generally been encouraged to believe—is inimical to the imagination.[15]

In a discussion of the poetry found in our hymnody—much of it third-rate—C. S. Lewis made this larger point about the relationship of theology to poetic expression:

As cleanliness and conveniences are the only beauties, other than those of the spirit, to which our Protestant churches aspire, so strong sense, rigid sincerity, genuine English, and the firmness of the metre shall be the only beauties of our sacred poetry— unless, indeed, a new uncovenanted beauty creeps in from the very contrast between the horrors or ecstasies described and the stern, unshaken lucidity of the form. . . . The heart may be broken but the head is clear. It is the method of Watts and the Wesleys at their best, of Cowper nearly always. It is divided by a hair's breadth from flatness; but when it comes off it can no more be ignored than the blow of a hammer.[16]

Lewis acknowledges "clean and straightforward" as characteristic of Protestantism, but his subsequent discussion shows that simplicity is not necessarily inimical to aesthetic beauty. Indeed, simplicity *is* an aesthetic value and can be used to great poetic effect. And that is something that Eliot himself was very capable of doing.

Francis Schaeffer used to refer to the "mannishness of man" and how it could not be entirely suppressed, whatever the worldview might be. Even when you take a theology that is manifestly deficient in scriptural terms—take the Shakers, for instance—you can still wind up with some great furniture at the end of the day. So we ought not to neglect the issues of worldview, but at the same time we don't want to be bigoted partisans—the kind of thought that can always win an argument by maintaining that Eliot would have been an even *greater* poet if he had only been a Southern Baptist, for example. Counterfactuals can frequently be a great deal of fun but are less frequently useful.

Great poetic genius can be born into the Catholic tradition (Hopkins), Anglicanism (Herbert), or Puritanism (Milton). And in that place they will create with the materials they find ready at hand. As one sage in the Old West put it, you play cards with the hand you are dealt. So the real test of a theology is not to find the solitary genius; the real test is when you find a *crop* of poets. The test of a theology is what kind of culture it builds. Henry Van Til once said that culture is religion externalized, and it seems that a better process would be to consider the culture generally and not just the solitary geniuses. And on that score, the Puritans did far better than they usually get credit for. "The number of good Puritan poets, as I have attempted to suggest in this study, is far larger than has been realized."[17] In this respect I have found the Puritans too easily disparaged, as I believe Howard unfortunately does here. But though he is wrong about the Puritans, I believe Howard is right about Eliot, and since we are talking about Eliot, we should let it rest there.

Doctrinal differences aside, Eliot shares something in common with all Christian poets who deal with the permanent things, with the great issues. To be a *Christian* poet is to be shaped by the central Christian story, which is a story of death and resurrection. Commenting on the relationship between Eliot and Dante, Peter Leithart notes this:

> Virgil leads him to the gate of Hell, where Dante will first descend before he can begin to ascend. Virgil's guidance is much like that of T.S. Eliot, who advised his modern readers, living in the dark world of the twentieth century, not to avoid the darkness. Instead, the way forward is to move from the partial darkness of the world to the utter darkness. In lines that doubtless allude to Dante (among others), Eliot counseled, "let the dark come upon you/which shall be the darkness of God."[18]

Let the dark come upon you. An old blues song says it this way: everybody wants to go to heaven, but nobody wants to die. There are no shortcuts to glory; God has determined that the route to glory runs straight through the center of *this* world. And because this world is under the sway of death and the attendant darkness, it is necessary to follow Christ in the way of death so that we might follow him in the way of resurrection. This is what our baptism *means*—death and resurrection. As many of us as were baptized, were baptized into his death, and this happened so that we might walk with him in newness of life. Baptized poets bring us baptized poetry, and that means poetry that goes through the grave and beyond. As George Herbert once put it, "Death used to be an executioner, but the gospel has made him just a gardener."[19]

For some, this was long ago relegated to the "dry doctrine room," but in novels and in poetry, it is that which makes the literary art *work*. Whether it is Aragorn taking the paths of the dead, or Beowulf grappling with Grendel's mother, or Chesterton taking on the early pessimistic Eliot, we see the necessity of both death and hope together.

Before his conversion, in *The Waste Land* and *The Hollow Men* Eliot did not see much hope, which is all to the good because without Christ, there is no hope. It is Christ or nothing. But in *The Hollow Men* Eliot's famous lines are these:

> This is the way the world ends
> Not with a bang but a whimper.

But Chesterton wasn't having any. In his essay *The Spice of Life* he said, "I recognize the great realities Mr. Eliot has revealed; but I do not admit that this is the deepest reality."[20] He also said this:

> Some sneer; some snigger; some simper;
> In the youth where we laughed and sang.
> And *they* may end with a whimper
> But *we* will end with a bang.[21]

I said a moment ago that it is Christ or nothing. Every form of idolatry is, in some sense, a form of nihilism. If I worship the true God, then I am worshiping the Ancient of Days, the eternal God. But if I worship any created thing whatsoever, I am serving something *that used to be nothing* (I am indebted to Tim Edwards for this point). God created the entire cosmos from nothing, and this means that if we go back far enough in the idol's lineage, we have come to the point where this god, whatever it might be, was not. What Arius falsely claimed about the Lord Jesus is true in this instance—there was a time when this was not. And anything that used to be nothing is nothing in principle now, held in existence by nothing other than the sheer pleasure and will and words of God (Col. 1:18). If the true God ceased speaking the created world, the created world would cease to be. The created world would then become the ex-world, or that which was formerly the world.

Despite his modernism of form, after his conversion Eliot became a true cultural conservative. He became a defender of the permanent things instead of one bidding a wistful farewell to those things that one might have wished could have been permanent. His poetry was part of a conversation that spanned centuries, and it became the best kind of contemporary poetry—the kind that carries the past into the future. That is what conservatism actually needs to do, does it not?

> Culture—distinguishable from knowledge about culture—was transmitted by the older universities. . . . But by far the most important channel of transmission of culture remains the family: and when family life fails to play its part, we must expect our culture to deteriorate. . . . When I speak of the family, I have in mind a bond which embraces a longer period of time than this: a piety toward the dead, however obscure, and a solicitude for the unborn, however remote.[22]

The human race is extended in time over generations because of fathers and mothers, grandfathers and grandmothers, not to mention the children who are all in the process of growing up into fathers and mothers and grandfathers and grandmothers. Teaching your children is therefore not an isolated act. You are teaching what you were taught by your father, who was taught when he was a boy. Culture is a river, and our neighbors upstream and downstream are very much our *neighbors*. This is the case even if they are several centuries upstream.

A couple today with five kids is thought to be normal in some places and outlandish in Manhattan, but still, the thing can be done.

I have three kids, and they have five kids, five kids, and six kids, the six kids breaking the tape ahead of the others because of twins. It is not an impossibility. But if each of those sixteen kids has five kids, we are now talking about eighty great-grandchildren, and my wife and I are starting to have birthday-card nightmares. If *they* have five kids each, we are dealing with four hundred souls. The point of this small math exercise is to show that after three more generations of this fecundity (two thousand, ten thousand, and fifty thousand), we are talking about something beyond a nuclear family. But the impact we may have on them can be profound and is focused in the discipleship of our children and children's children. I have often told parents that they are (most likely), in the providence of God, ancestors of hundreds of thousands of people. Not only so, but we and all our hundreds of thousands of tenth cousins are all descendants of a happy couple who met several centuries ago on market day in their village.

Honoring our parents (and ancestors) does not need to reduce to mere tribalism. Loving and nourishing our distant children is not superstition. Eliot shows us the way in this kind of thinking.

One of the ways of reaching future descendants is through poetry, but the way this reaches them is mysterious.

> For I think it is important that every people should have its own poetry, not simply for those who enjoy poetry—such people could always learn other languages and enjoy their poetry—but because it actually makes a difference to the society as a whole, and that means to people who do not enjoy poetry. I include even those who do not know the names of their own national poets.[23]

Eliot says it is comparatively easy to learn to *think* in another language, but it really takes some doing to learn how to *feel* in another language.[24] People don't want to replace their native language with another language because they don't want to become someone else.[25] This is why poetry is the most stubbornly national of all the arts,[26] an art that is given to each of us in the medium we learned from our fathers and mothers. An art with deeper roots in the native soil.

Eliot was a conservative Christian, an incarnational Christian, and this anchors him to *place*. *Little Gidding* comes to mind. This is not mere jingoism; religious sensibilities can be imparted only with words, and words belong to particular languages. Those languages, in order to function as real languages, must have poets to express, exalt, and refine them.

> Much has been said everywhere about the decline of religious belief; not so much notice has been taken of the decline of religious sensibility. The trouble of the modern age is not merely the inability to believe certain things about God and man which our forefathers believed, but the inability to *feel* towards God and man as they did. A belief in which you no longer believe is something which to some extent you can still understand; but when religious feeling disappears, the words in which men have struggled to express it become meaningless.[27]

The poet is preserving the atmosphere in which the words of the gospel can be spoken. The true poet is keeping alive the possibility that words will still be able to do in the future what only the Word can do. But even the Word will be silent in a vacuum. The apostle Paul does not disparage the necessary preconditions to communication. How will they hear without a preacher, and how will he preach unless he is sent? Extend the same principle further. How will they hear if they haven't learned how to listen to ordinary speech? How will they hear of heavenly things if they haven't had their imaginations prepared by the poets?

A good poet commands respect over time. This is one of the definitions of a classic—it wears well. A poet can generate excitement in his own day (or perhaps not), but that is largely beside the point. In fact, "if a poet gets a large audience very quickly, that is a rather suspicious circumstance."[28]

As Eliot put it, "It matters little whether a poet had a large audience in his own time. What matters is that there should always be at least a small audience for him in every generation."[29] Eliot's death was almost a half century ago, and all the early returns indicate that by this measure, he will continue to contribute to "the great conversation" over generations.

IF YOU READ NOTHING ELSE

Eliot made his first real mark with *The Love Song of J. Alfred Prufrock* (1917), a poem that is sardonic, amusing, and cynical. He became the voice of that lost generation (or so they thought) with the publication of *The Waste Land* (1922), considered to be central to the canon of modernist poetry. But while most of the bleak prophets of grim were busy prophesying their way out of the modern world into something pretty vapid, Eliot was actually headed the other direction—conversion to the Christian faith.

He published *Ash Wednesday* (1930), his first long poem after his conversion. He was also a playwright and published *Murder in the Cathedral* (1935). His poetic masterpiece was *Four Quartets* (1935–1942).

For those who want a taste of his reasoning, and his prose, I would recommend his *Christianity and Culture* and a collection of essays called *On Poetry and Poets*.

5

J. R. R. Tolkien

A WRITER'S LIFE

J. R. R. Tolkien had a problem, along with C. S. Lewis, and as we should also, with sentences that begin like this. But Tolkien also had a problem with people who tried to understand works of literature as simple extensions of biography. He objected strongly to the idea that literary criticism could be legitimately grounded in the life experiences of the author.

At the same time, we cannot simply dismiss the outline of someone's life as irrelevant to the work they do. An author is more than a simple pipeline or conduit for inspirations from the beyond. How Tolkien lived his life, his worldview, and what influenced him are all relevant in understanding his stories, although in deference to Tolkien we have to grant that they are not deterministic.

Tolkien was born in South Africa in 1892, the son of an English banker, in the town of Bloemfontein. His father died tragically while his four-year-old son was visiting England with his mother. After his father's death, there was no reason to return to South Africa, and so Mabel, his mother, decided to remain in England, which is where he and his brother Hilary grew up.

Earlier in Africa, when he was first beginning to walk, he was bitten by a tarantula and ran terrified to a nurse who sucked out the poison. He said this left him with no particular fear of spiders, but we may wonder if perhaps it left him with a peculiar awareness of them? For anyone who was going to invent Shelob later, it should have. Biographical details do make a difference. Tolkien and his brother were once chased out of a field by a farmer they called the "Black Ogre," who was angry at them for picking his mushrooms. A nearby inventor of cotton wool dressing was named Dr. Gamgee, and so cotton wool was called *gamgee*. Reading Tolkien's biography reveals a number of obvious connections between his life and certain events in his stories.

Though Tolkien grew up without a father, he flourished under the influence of a gracious, cultivated mother. The small family was not wealthy, but his mother knew Latin, French, and German and had an artistic bent. Tolkien, as we all know now, was brilliant and had the kind of upbringing that could frequently leave him alone with his own thoughts, including, in his case, his own invented languages. He loved the sounds of words.

In 1900 his mother was received into the Roman Catholic Church, which caused great tension in her Protestant Suffield family. In fact, Tolkien blamed her early death on the treatment she received at their hands. He actually considered her a martyr, and this also helps explain his wholehearted devotion to the Roman church and his antipathy toward the Church of England. Personal loyalties are not always a matter of rational calculus.

At King Edward's School in Birmingham, Tolkien developed a friendship with Christopher Wiseman, a son of a Methodist minister. Both were gifted Latin and Greek scholars, and both were what we Americans call "jocks." They were fierce rugby players. During this time, Tolkien made his acquaintance with Anglo-Saxon, a language that combines in a strange way the familial and the remote—both characteristics of Tolkien's writing.

He met Edith Bratt at this time, his future wife. They were separated for three years before Tolkien could pursue his interest in her. He was Beren; she was Luthien.

The schoolboys formed the TC, BS (Tea Club, Barrovian Society). It was called this because they had tea when they met, and for a time they met in Barrow's Stores. Tolkien and Wiseman and another boy named Gilson, along with some others, had a deep sense of their own mission. They were not far wrong, and this same mentality surfaces again with the Inklings. One anecdote from that era tells a tale of remarkable ability:

> There was a custom at King Edward's of holding a debate entirely in Latin, but that was almost too easy for Tolkien, and in one debate when taking the role of Greek Ambassador to the Senate he spoke entirely in Greek. On another occasion he astonished his schoolfellows when, in the character of a barbarian envoy, he broke into fluent Gothic; and on a third occasion he spoke in Anglo-Saxon.[1]

Tolkien married Edith just before he shipped out to serve in the First World War. The war is significant, in my view, for two things. First, it represented the breaking of the great schoolboy fellowship; the fellowship dispersed, just as it did in *The Lord of the Rings*. Rob Gilson was killed in action. Smith was killed. Great men were once boys, but boys sometimes know they will be great men. Others from his schoolboy company fell in battle, but Tolkien had a sense of destiny.

The other great thing was that Tolkien got a closeup view of the machinery of modern warfare. The front lines of that war may be considered as the inspiration for Mordor. The American War between the States was the first post–Industrial Revolution war, but the First World War was the first modern war on such a grand scale. Tolkien never forgot what he called the "animal horror" of trench warfare. The modern age *clanks*, *grinds*, *and devours*, and especially in time of war.

After the war, Tolkien got his first academic position at Leeds. He helped put the English department there on the map. But when a position opened at Oxford in 1925, a professorship in Anglo-Saxon, Tolkien applied for it and was accepted. Tolkien's interest in this subject was far more than academic; it was a religious issue for him. This can be misunderstood, so let us use the term *lifeview*, or *worldview*.

Without a doubt, Lewis was Tolkien's closest friend over the course of his lifetime. When they met, neither was a stranger to the world of close emotional and intellectual friendships, but at the same time, they were particularly suited to one another. Because of this, we can learn a great deal about each from the other one.

The college of English at Oxford was divided into two factions: the language and the literature factions. Lewis was in the lit group, and Tolkien, as the professor of Anglo-Saxon, was lang. The situation was ameliorated somewhat by the fact that Lewis was a medievalist, but still, there it was. After he met Tolkien, Lewis wrote in his diary: "No harm in him, only needs a smack or so."[2] The friendship began in earnest in 1927 when Tolkien recruited Lewis into the Coalbiters, a group he established so that folks could learn Icelandic.

Lewis, though brilliant, was still a generalist. Tolkien, though a lover of the forest, was a close enough scholar to see the trees. Lewis was not a perfectionist, and Tolkien was. As Lewis put it in a comment on how Tolkien reacted to criticism of his writing, "Either he begins the whole work over again from the beginning or he takes no notice at all."[3]

These differences are notable in their production. Lewis could simply crank it out. Tolkien's production was painstakingly slow, *The Lord of the Rings* being produced over many years. A reader of Tolkien's *Letters* will note that Tolkien agonized over making sure that the phases of the moon were not contradictory in the chronologies. Lewis would sit down, lick his pencil, and *Io! Triumphum!* But Lewis loved the fruit of Tolkien's labors. This is what he said in a review of *The Hobbit*: "Everything in it so ripe, so friendly, and in its own way so true."[4]

Their shared love of myth was at the foundation of their friendship and also the basis of Lewis's conversion. Before he was converted, Lewis thought that myths were "lies breathed through silver." But there was one fateful night when Tolkien and Hugo Dyson had a lengthy talk with Lewis, in which they showed him that *myth* need not be equated with *false*.

Lewis had become a theist by 1929 but was not yet a Christian. As a result of this talk, Lewis came to see that the story of Christ was true myth. As words are invented to speak to real objects, so myths are invented to address the realities beyond. As some words are more felicitous than others, so are some myths. The Christian myth is no myth at all, in the popular understanding of the word *myth*.

Tolkien wrote in his diary, "Friendship with Lewis compensates for much . . . a man at once honest, brave, intellectual—a scholar, a poet, a philosopher—and a lover, at least after a long pilgrimage, of Our Lord."[5]

The reason they drifted (relatively) apart later in life was most probably a combination of Tolkien's curmudgeonliness and Lewis's deepening Protestantism. The former may have had something to do with jealousy over Lewis's friendship with Charles Williams, which began in the late thirties. But do not take this as the result of a fracas or falling out or any dislike of Williams personally by Tolkien. The two of them were friends as well.

The latter reason was no doubt complex as well. The context of it was how Lewis had become a very famous apologist for the Christian faith. Not only so, but he did this as a Protestant.

Lewis had been brought up an Ulster Protestant; his nurse had once warned him against stepping in a puddle full of "wee, nastie popes." As Lewis grew and matured in his Christian life, he grew increasingly committed to the Protestant faith. What had been his default position became a matter of deep conviction. Tolkien said, "He would become again a Northern Ireland Protestant."[6]

Near the end of Lewis's life, with the publication of his magnum opus, *English Literature in the Sixteenth Century*, Tolkien was irritated by the fact that Lewis called Catholics "papists" and that he praised Calvin and Tyndale, etc. And he did: "the dazzling figure of Calvin."[7]

Under those conditions formulae might possibly have been found which did justice to the Protestant—I had almost said the Pauline—assertions without compromising . . .[8]

From this buoyant humility, this farewell to the self with all its good resolutions, anxiety, scruples, and motive-scratchings, all the Protestant doctrines originally sprang.[9]

By the time I had really explained my objection to certain doctrines which differentiate you from us (and also in my opinion from the Apostolic and even the Medieval Church), you would like me less.[10]

Throughout the letters of Tolkien, we see references to him reading his stuff to Lewis and other friends. (Their dependence was, of course, mutual.) This was usually done under the auspices of the Inklings. "I hope to see C.S.L. and Charles W. tomorrow morning and read my next chapter."[11] The Inklings had no formal membership and was mostly a gathering of literary male friends around Lewis, who were all Christians.

DIGGING DEEPER

Both Lewis and Tolkien have been greatly misunderstood because people have assumed that they know what the men were attempting to do. But if you put a work of fiction into the wrong category, a lot of confusion can result and, in this case, has. The main confusion that has to be cleared up has to do with the matter of allegory.

The Lord of the Rings is not allegory. Speaking of *The Hobbit*, Tolkien says, "Though it is not an allegory."[12] Neither are the Narnia stories an allegory. So what *is* allegory, and if they are not allegory, what are these stories then?

First, Tolkien recognizes the problem we face. He said:

I dislike Allegory—the conscious and intentional allegory—yet any attempt to explain the purport of the myth or fairy tale must use allegorical language. (And, of course, the more "life" a story has the more readily will it be susceptible of allegorical interpretations: while the better a deliberate allegory is made the more nearly will it be acceptable just as a story.) Anyway, all this stuff is mainly concerned with Fall, Mortality, and the Machine.[13]

And elsewhere he says this:

> Do not let Rayner suspect "Allegory." There is a "moral," I suppose, in any tale worth telling. But that is not the same thing. . . . Of course, Allegory and Story converge, meeting somewhere in Truth. So that the only perfectly consistent allegory is a real life; and the only fully intelligible story is an allegory. . . . You can make the Ring into an allegory of our own time, if you like: an allegory of the inevitable fate that waits for all attempts to defeat evil power by power.[14]

Our problem is that we must traffic in definitional subtleties. According to Lewis, every metaphor is an "allegory in little."[15] The "twilight of the gods is the mid-morning of the personifications."[16] Tolkien and Lewis were working on an important "project" together, and so it is important for us to get this right.

> This fundamental equivalence between the immaterial and the material may be used by the mind in two ways. . . . On the one hand you can start with an immaterial fact, such as the passions which you actually experience, and can then invent *visibilia* to express them. If you are hesitating between an angry retort and a soft answer, you can express your state of mind by inventing a person called *Ira* with a torch and letting her contend with another invented person called *Patientia*. This is allegory . . . but there is another way of using the equivalence, which is almost the opposite of allegory, and which I would call sacramentalism or symbolism. . . . The attempt to read that something else through its sensible imitations, to see the archetype in the copy, is what I mean by symbolism or sacramentalism.[17]

If Aslan represented the immaterial Deity in the same way in which Giant Despair represents despair, he would be an allegorical figure. In reality however he is an invention giving an imaginary answer to the question, "What might Christ become like, if there really were a world like Narnia and He chose to be incarnate and die and rise again in that world as He actually has done in ours?" This is not allegory at all.[18]

The Pilgrim's Regress is allegory. *The Great Divorce* is symbolism. *The Lord of the Rings* and the Narnia stories are subcreated (a word that Tolkien coined) and mythopoeic realms.

Subcreation does not necessarily mean another universe entirely. Middle-earth was meant to be mythology for England, and Narnia is connected to England by "tunnels" and has English children running around in it. Subcreation means a "world" of events over which an author presides in the place of God. In short, it refers to what we call fiction but does not include what we think of fiction, i.e., falsehood.

In the world Tolkien created, he successfully achieved the "donegality" of true northernness. That word *donegality* was coined by Lewis (describing the "feel" of County Donegal) and used by Michael Ward to describe the atmosphere that Lewis successfully achieved in his Narniad. But Tolkien achieved a very similar donegality, different from Narnia but equally northern.

C. S. Lewis described this as related to a longing or *Sehnsucht*.[19] As he develops it, it should be understood as a creaturely longing for eternity. Considered from another angle it is autumn as an *idea*.[20] A third term for it is *northernness*, and this may take some explaining. Lewis was once reading Longfellow, and:

When I idly turned the pages of the book and found the un-rhymed translation of *Tegner's Drapa* and read

I heard a voice that cried,
Balder the beautiful
Is dead, is dead—

I knew nothing about Balder; but instantly I was uplifted into huge regions of northern sky, I desired with almost sickening intensity something never to be described (except that it is cold, spacious, severe, pale, and remote) and then, as in the other examples, found myself at the very same moment already falling out of that desire and wishing I were back in it.[21]

Although Tolkien was a different personality type from Lewis, this description of northernness fits the work of Tolkien very well and indicates that much the same thing was going on in his affections. Consider the words *cold, spacious, severe, pale, and remote* as descriptive of the world in *The Lord of the Rings*. They cover just about everything except the Shire—which is necessary for dramatic purposes—something to give us traction.

You can see this shared element in how Lewis described his response to *The Lord of the Rings*: "Here are beauties which pierce like swords or burn like cold iron; here is a book that will break your heart."[22] Whatever else we may say about northernness and Tolkien, we can say that Tolkien's work evoked the response of northernness in Lewis.

But we do not just see this reflecting off Lewis. Tolkien had more than a little to say about himself directly. He comments on his daughter's experience with Chesterton:

[Priscilla] has been wading through *The Ballad of the White Horse* for the last many nights; and my efforts to explain the obscurer parts to her convince me that it is not as good as I thought. The ending is absurd. The brilliant smash and glitter of the words and phrases (when they come off, and are not mere loud colors) cannot disguise the fact that G.K.C. knew nothing whatever about the "North", heathen or Christian.[23]

Tolkien's affinity for the north was fundamentally linguistic. He was a gifted philologist, and his love of language was what made his motor run. He commented on the impact this had on *The Hobbit*: "The magic and mythology and assumed 'history' and most of the names. . . . I believe they give the narrative an air of 'reality' and have a northern atmosphere."[24]

Tolkien wanted to write a mythology that he could "dedicate simply to: to England; to my country. It should possess the tone and quality that I desire, somewhat cool and clear, be redolent of our 'air' (the clime and soil of the North West, meaning Britain and the hither parts of Europe: not Italy or the Aegean, still less the East), and, while possessing (if I could achieve it) the fair elusive beauty that some call Celtic (though it is rarely found in genuine ancient Celtic things), it should be 'high', purged of the gross, and fit for the more adult mind of a land long now steeped in poetry."[25]

So then, in developing this world, Tolkien attributed it to linguistics, his passionate love for growing things, and "the deep response to legends (for lack of a better word) that have what I would call the North-western temper and temperature."[26] This includes far more than lots of snow; it includes a vast ocean to the west and enemies from the east.

But, of course, anything so lovely as the north is going to have, in this fallen world at any rate, temptations that come with it and suggested counterfeits. Lewis pointed to this problem when he has Dr. Dimble in *That Hideous Strength* going on and on about Logres. But every nation has its own Logres. No jingoism here. Tolkien dealt with it this way: "Auden has asserted that for me 'the North is a sacred direction'. That is not true. The North-west of Europe, where I (and most of my ancestors) have lived, has my affection, as a man's home should. I love its atmosphere . . . but it is not sacred."[27] But there is still an *idea* here.

The potency of that idea is seen in Tolkien's reactions to the Aryan counterfeit, what he called "Furor Teutonicus." He said:

Anyway, I have in this War a burning private grudge—which would probably make me a better soldier at 49 than I was at 22: against that ruddy little ignoramus Adolf Hitler (for the odd thing about demonic inspiration and impetus is that it in no way enhances the purely intellectual stature: it chiefly affects the mere will). Ruining, perverting, misapplying, and making for ever accursed, that noble northern spirit, a supreme contribution to Europe, which I have ever loved, and tried to present in its true light. Nowhere, incidentally, was it nobler than in England, nor more early sanctified and Christianized.[28]

In Tolkien's mind, the north was nothing without nobility. In his great essay "Beowulf: The Monsters and the Critics," Tolkien said this: "The high tone, the sense of dignity, alone is evidence in Beowulf of the presence of a mind lofty and thoughtful."[29] Later he says, "One of the most potent elements in that fusion is the Northern courage: the theory of courage, which is the great contribution of early Northern literature. . . . I refer rather to the central position the creed of unyielding will holds in the North."[30] In this ancient view, defeat is no refutation. All the good guys go down at Ragnarok, but this does not mean they were wrong. This view was picked up and *transformed* by the Christian vision but not reversed. Heaven awaits, but earthly history is still grim. We have an early, noble amillennialism.

For Tolkien, the north embodied certain human virtues in a similar way as the elves did. He was not so foolish to believe that character altered with the latitude. Northernness is a metaphor (and a very effective one) to describe a certain frame of heart and mind. And that frame was: courageous against all odds, gracious, aesthetically sensitive, kind, bold, in love with the good, loyal, and shrewd, adept and creative in artisanship—in short, noble.

> Now the heroic figures, the men of old, *haeleth under heofenum*, remained and still fought on until defeat. For the monsters do not depart, whether the gods go or come. A Christian was (and is) still like his forefathers a mortal hemmed in a hostile world. . . . The tragedy of the great temporal defeat remains for a while poignant, but ceases to be finally important.[31]

Having described this northern donegality, a few other things can be set in place in that context, things like magic and technology, Christian theology and eucatastrophic endings. Just a few remaining ends and odds.

An interesting contrast between art and technology is found in Tolkien. Magic for him was not a matter of wizards who "chirp and mutter," to use Isaiah's taunt. Remember that Gandalf was an angelic being, not a wizard in our sense. For Tolkien, machinery that clanks and smokes was always wicked. Frictionless technology, magic, was not magic, not science, but art. Authority in the world through art was noble, and domination through machinery was, in his mind, ignoble.

Treebeard says of Saruman that he "has a mind of metal and wheels; and he does not care for growing things." Gandalf says to Saruman, "He that breaks a thing to find out what it is has left the path of wisdom."

The questions about art and technology are also closely related to the issue of magic. Some Christians have been troubled by the wizardry, but the whole point of magic is the manipulation of matter in order to acquire power, which is what an ordinary magician does, becoming an adept. But the world of *The Lord of the Rings* is the very reverse of this—the good guys there represent a photo negative of magic. The ring of power is the ultimate symbol of magic in the traditional sense, and the whole point of the book is to destroy it, resisting all temptations to use it. All such temptations are temptations, in effect, to engage in what we would call "white magic."

A key element in the fairy story was the ending, and Tolkien found that he needed a term to describe what was going on. That word was *eucatastrophe*. Not surprisingly, this is connected to the resurrection of Jesus. "And I concluded by saying that the Resurrection was the greatest 'eucatastrophe' possible in the greatest Fairy Story."[32]

> Almost I would venture to assert that all complete fairy stories must have it. At least I would say that Tragedy is the true form of Drama, its highest function; but the opposite is true of Fairy-story. Since we do not appear to possess a word that expresses this opposite—I will call it Eucatastrophe. The eucatastrophic tale is the true form of fairy-tale, and its highest function.[33]

The Christian joy, the *Gloria*, is of the same kind; but it is preeminently (infinitely, if our capacity were not finite) high and joyous. Because this story is supreme; and it is true. Art has been verified. God is the Lord, of angels, and of men—and of elves. Legend and History have met and fused.[34]

What about the key theological concepts—God, man, sin, salvation, and revelation? Part of the problem that Tolkien had with the Arthurian stories is that they were explicitly set within the Christian era, and this made the "remoteness" he wanted for dramatic reasons impossible. The long-ago-ness and far-away-ness would not have been long or far enough away for him. But God was not excluded because of any theological embarrassment. Tolkien wanted everything remote in time. Here is Lewis on that element: "But in the Tolkienian world you can hardly put your foot down anywhere from Esgaroth to Forlindon or between Ered Mithrin and Khand, without stirring the dust of history."[35]

At the ultimate level in the mythology (in the *Silmarillion*), God necessarily fills the place that only he can fill—Illuvatar. He is the creator. But even here, he hands off the details of creation to the Valar. But notice how Tolkien solves another problem with this, the problem of having God occupy the role of a *character* in a fictional world created by one of us. Lewis solved this same problem (with Aslan) by having the connotative images (using a lion) different enough so that we wouldn't stumble over it.

In Tolkien's work, mankind (without using the language) clearly bears the *imago Dei*. Illuvatar has given man the gift of death, a gift that the Elves envy. Something special is occurring between God and men, and what that might be is never expressly stated. And speaking of Elves, this shows how *complex* Tolkien's view of mankind is. The only "children" of Middle-earth who are not men in some way are the dwarves. The Hobbits are men. "The Hobbits are, of course, really meant to be a branch of the specifically human race."[36] This is why they can dwell with the Big Folk at Bree. They represent the sturdy heroism of ordinary men. What about the Elves? They are biologically one with men and can intermarry—and do. "Elves and Men are represented as biologically akin in this 'history', because Elves are certain aspects of Men and their talents and desires, incarnated in my little world."[37] In short, they are the incarnation of nobility—beauty, sorrow, wisdom, authority. They represent "beauty and grace of life and artifact."[38] They are a representation of a part of human nature.[39] If "I were pressed to rationalize, I should say that they represent really Men with greatly enhanced aesthetic and creative faculties, greater beauty and longer life, *and nobility*."[40] Orcs must therefore be corruptions,[41] and, as Tolkien put it, "Elves may turn into orcs."[42] This means of course (given what Elves are) that orcs are representations of man's potential for sin. Tolkien goes so far as to say that many men "to be met today" are as horribly corrupted as the orcs are.[43] And, of course, the men are men. No need for any detailed argumentation here, I suppose.

The portrayal of sin is one of Tolkien's great strengths. Below Illuvatar, sin is possible at every level and does occur at every level. Among the Valar, Morgoth sins. The Elves seek after forbidden knowledge, and their presence in Middle-earth is the result of their "fall." The complete corruption of orcs shows how far the process can go. Even Galadriel is a penitent. Men, of course, sin. Hobbits fall in with Saruman to corrupt the Shire, and Gollum is how Hobbits go to the orcs. The "good guys" are not without their complexities and corruptions. Lewis put it this way: "Heroic Rohan and imperial Gondor are partly diseased."[44] Tolkien has no patience with the relativism of our age. Aragon says that "good and ill have not changed since yesteryear" and that they are not "one thing among Elves and Dwarves and another among Men."

On the flip side, I would have to say that this is Tolkien's weakest point. Salvation appears to be accepted on all hands as a matter of simple repentance. There appears to be no sense of a need for *atonement*. In Narnia, Aslan has to die. But here? Morgoth sins up a storm and then gets off the hook by feigning repentance. Sauron feigns repentance. Gollum comes within a step of repentance. But suppose true repentance. Then what? What about the millions of murders? Tolkien could defend his position by saying the repentance was feigned, but this presupposes a basis among the good for accepting it.

Nevertheless, despite this failing, the Christian ethos is very strong. Rather, consider the comment of Elrond: "This quest may be attempted by the weak with as much hope as the strong. Yet such is oft the course of deeds that move the wheels of the world: small hands do them because they must, while the eyes of the great are elsewhere." The first will be last and the last will be first. God has chosen the weak things of this world to confound the strong. Or, as Frodo says at the Grey Havens, some give things up so that others may have them.

IF YOU READ NOTHING ELSE

I love Tolkien's world and want to commend it to you. But I would like to do this in a way that leans against the temptation of Middle-earth geekdom, which memorizes all the genealogies in *The Silmarillion*. I am glad Tolkien wrote it, because it was essential to his creative process of writing. But I really don't think you need to read it more than once.

I would recommend reading *The Hobbit* and *The Lord of the Rings* at recurring intervals throughout your life. They are just glorious.

For those who want a background glimpse into Tolkien's mind, his collected *Letters* (Carpenter) are very informative. *Leaf by Niggle* and *Farmer Giles of Ham* are both fun but don't draw you back to them time and again the way Middle-earth does.

Of course, we cannot really talk about *The Lord of the Rings* anymore without talking about the movies and why they should be avoided. If someone is introduced to the books because he saw the movies first, this is simply one more testimony as to how God in his sovereignty can bring good out of evil. But I do not think any traffic should go the other direction, from the books to the movies.

I think the first movie was the only one I finished all the way through. But from that limited exposure, let me just put some of the irritations into one paragraph and be done. Maybe it was because they couldn't find the appropriate place in New Zealand, but the plains of Rohan were way too rocky. I had trouble with Aragorn floating in the river, getting kissed by his horse, and all surrounded by a major Enja moment. The village (!) of Rohan evacuating was like a Monty Python view of what it was to live in medieval-like settings. The fact that elves came to defend Helm's Deep was bad enough, but to have them arrive like a precision marching drill team was the utter frozen limit. Legolas sliding down the stairs on a shield or something was a nice James Bond treatment. In the final sortie at Helm's Deep, I was interested to learn where the horses suddenly came from. Mordor looked like a Transylvanian castle on Halloween night, on steroids. *Way* overdone. In the category of the overdone, I would also want to list Gandalf's theophany. Way too bright. I would also put Theoden's release from his spell here. And Wormtongue was just a tad more greasy than Aragorn. Am I impossible to please? No. Good job on Gollum. Just right, in fact.

6

C. S. Lewis

A WRITER'S LIFE

In *That Hideous Strength*, Dr. Dimble sees a student coming up the walk, and the student was, I am afraid, a dullard. Dr. Dimble sighed in resignation and said the student was the sort who would begin an essay on Jonathan Swift by saying, "Swift was born . . ."

But this is the *second* paragraph, and so C. S. Lewis was born in 1899 in Belfast, Northern Ireland. He died in 1963, on the same day that President Kennedy was shot. He died a week before his sixty-fifth birthday. His friends knew him as Jack, a nickname he had bestowed on himself as a toddler.

When he was ten years old, his mother died, an event that affected him profoundly, both emotionally and practically. It resulted in a missing buffer between Lewis and his father, which had additional ramifications for his time away at boarding schools. Some of those experiences at school were pretty rough. And it is clear that the loss of his mother was something he carried with him through life, as a thoughtful reading of *The Magician's Nephew* makes clear. Digory's feelings about his mother's illness was something that Lewis knew from the inside out very well.

In the course of growing up, he first attempted to live a Christian life of ultra sincerity, a misguided effort that kept collapsing on itself. Eventually he drifted into atheism, repudiating the faith he had been brought up in. He eventually escaped a miserable boarding school situation and was tutored by the "Great Knock," a man named Kirkpatrick, an experience in which Lewis was able to thrive. It was here that his rational and logical capacities were hardened, and this, when combined with his creative and literary gifts, created a true romantic rationalist. Kirkpatrick was an atheist but was used by God to train and educate one of the most effective apologists for the Christian faith.

In *Surprised by Joy* Lewis alludes to his service in the Army during the First World War. He was dismissive of the whole affair, saying that he was willing to go fight and die in battles, but he was not willing to read about such battles beforehand. But he did go, was wounded by shrapnel, and returned to England.

After the war, in 1925, he received a teaching fellowship at Magdalen College, Oxford. He soon met J. R. R. Tolkien, and though he was wary at first, they rapidly became close friends. When he first met him, he wrote in his diary that Tolkien was a "smooth, pale, fluent little chap. . . . No harm in him: only needs a smack or so." But they were soon deep into the mysteries of friendship. Tolkien invited Lewis to join a group called the Coalbiters, which (as we noted earlier) specialized in reading Icelandic myths—in the original. The idea of the name was to call up an image of Icelandic Vikings, sitting around a fire through a long winter, "biting the coal," and telling each other stories. This friendship between Tolkien and Lewis became the heart of another, more famous group, the Inklings, which provided edifying stimulation to a group of writers over the course of many years. That was a literary group that helped to shape the twentieth century.

As a result of his friendship with Tolkien, Lewis was soon drawn back to the Christian faith. His return was reluctant but steady. He returned to theism first, and then some time after, he concluded that Jesus was the Son of God. A key element in his return was his love of myth and Tolkien's point that the faith was of course mythical. But why should that mean that it wasn't *true*?

During the Second World War, Lewis gave a series of broadcasts for the BBC called *The Case for Christianity*. These talks were the antecedent for the book *Mere Christianity*, which was an astoundingly successful apologetic for the truth of the Christian religion. In years following the war, Lewis developed three major careers, and he was a roaring success in all three. The first was in his chosen profession. He was an Oxford don, and in his professional field he contributed mightily. Books like *Allegory of Love* and *English Literature in the Sixteenth Century* fall into this category. The second field was that of lay theologian. He wrote for the common man, and he "made righteousness readable." His works of popular theology fall into this class—he was serving as a translator. He was a highly educated layman who could read theology and restate it in language that average men and women could understand. This includes books like *The Problem of Pain*; *Miracles*; and *Mere Christianity*, and at the very popular end of this spectrum, *The Great Divorce* and *The Screwtape Letters*. And the third field was that of fiction, his seven Narnia stories and what has perversely come to be known as the Space Trilogy: *Out of the Silent Planet*; *Perelandra*; and *That Hideous Strength*. I say "perversely" because a central reason he had for writing that trilogy was to get people to stop thinking of the heavens as "space."

In 1952 C. S. Lewis met his unlikely future wife, Joy. It was unlikely for various reasons: she was American, she was Jewish, and she was married. Her marriage had been marred by her husband's numerous infidelities; she had been converted to Christianity, in part helped by Lewis's writing; but nothing could be done about her being American. She was brilliant, an accomplished poet and novelist, and had a supple mind that could keep up with Lewis. She returned to the States in order to attempt a reconciliation with her husband, but he wanted a divorce, so she came back to England in November of 1953. I was five months old at the time, but that doesn't really enter into it.

After she came back to England, their friendship continued. But in 1956, her visa expired, which meant that she had to return to America, so Lewis married her in a civil ceremony to keep her in England. When she was diagnosed with cancer, later that same year, Jack realized that he was in love with her, and they were married in a Christian ceremony in 1957. Because she had been divorced, this posed a problem for the Church of England at that time, but it was nevertheless arranged, and an Anglican priest performed the ceremony. After treatment, she was able to go home, and the cancer went into remission. They enjoyed several years together, but the cancer returned in 1959, and she died the following year. After her passing, Lewis wrote a poignant record of his devastation entitled *A Grief Observed*, which was published under the false name of N. W. Clerk. This was a treatment of the "problem of pain" from an entirely different angle. That book is a tribute to his beloved wife and an account of how his faith staggered by the loss but then, suitably chastened, recovered. All this occurred three years before C. S. Lewis himself died.

DIGGING DEEPER

In order to understand the mainspring of C. S. Lewis's creativity, we should begin where he did, with the idea of aching after joy. Fundamental to Lewis's thought and life was this idea of longing or *Sehnsucht*. But this was not any old longing or desire; it had a peculiar character. "They taught me longing—*Sehnsucht*; made me for good or ill, and before I was six years old, a votary of the Blue Flower."[1] The blue flower was a symbol of the German romantic movement. From a Christian vantage point, we can see this is a creaturely longing for eternity. What happens when you try to put eternity into a human life? The same thing as when you try to put the Pacific Ocean into a thimble, only worse.

We are not parsing the grammar of a sentence or chopping logic (although that will come and has its place). As we will see, Lewis was more than a romantic, but he was certainly not less. So consider autumn as an *idea*:

It troubled me with what I can only describe as the Idea of Autumn. It sounds fantastic to say that one can be enamoured of a season, but that is something like what happened; and, as before, the experience was one of intense desire.[2]

We addressed this in the previous chapter with regard to Tolkien, but there is no way to avoid dealing with it again. Tolkien and Lewis were close friends, and close friends for a reason. They were both sons of the north, and theirs was a shared project.

I knew nothing about Balder; but instantly I was uplifted into huge regions of northern sky, I desired with almost sickening intensity something never to be described (except that it is cold, spacious, severe, pale, and remote) and then, as in the other examples, found myself at the very same moment already falling out of that desire and wishing I were back in it.[3]

Sehnsucht. Autumn. Northernness. Words don't do justice to something that is not about words at all. Combine all this, and we have an ineffable yearning, which is somehow connected (for Lewis) with a season and a hemisphere. But what kind of sense does that make? Another word for it all, developed by Rudolph Otto in his *The Idea of the Holy*—a book that Lewis appreciated very much—is the idea of the *numinous.* Here it is, in another place. In *The Weight of Glory* Lewis says this:

We want something else which can hardly be put into words— to be united with the beauty we see, to pass into it, to receive it into ourselves, to bathe in it, to become part of it. . . . We cannot mingle with the splendors we see. But all the leaves of the New Testament are rustling with the rumour that it will not always be so. Some day, God willing, we shall get *in.*[4]

God has put eternity in our hearts, so shall we define it and then pin it to a card, like it was a dead beetle? At the same time, and for precisely this reason, we must guard against (as Lewis himself guarded against) this element being turned into a false alternative to careful thought. Lewis was a romantic rationalist, and this fusion—the word *combination* is far too pedestrian—is a crucial element of his success as a writer.

This glorious fusion of two usually disparate traits occurred in Lewis in quite a remarkable way. His attraction to *Sehnsucht*, taken alone, would have given us Lewis the romantic. His abilities in logical reasoning, developed under his tutor Kirkpatrick, taken alone, would have resulted in an arid rationalism. The marriage of these two in Lewis resulted in something remarkable—something we need lots more of—Christian romantic rationalists, and may their tribe increase. I would refer you to an essay of Lewis's in *Christian Reflections* entitled "The Poison of Subjectivism,"[5] in which he shows a holy impatience with the kind of goo-thought that has inundated the modern world. But he does not react to this kind of subjectivism by joining up with the "men without chests."

As just mentioned, the concept of the numinous was developed by Rudolph Otto in his work *The Idea of the Holy*. The true God, worshiped insipidly, appears to be no God at all. False gods, disbelieved, and yet still numinous in a literary way, have a deep appeal—at least to someone with Lewis's sensibilities. Consider what Lewis said about this:

> We are taught in the Prayer Book to "give thanks to God for His great glory," as if we owed Him more thanks for being what He necessarily is than for any particular benefit He confers upon us; and so indeed we do and to know God is to know this. But I had been far from any such experience; I came far nearer to feeling this about the Norse gods whom I disbelieved in than I had ever done about the true God while I believed.[6]

False religions sometimes provide, under the sovereignty of God, training wheels for real faith, which necessitates careful thinking about natural law and common grace. Incidentally, for those who have eyes to see, we can see traces of Lewis's old teacher Kirkpatrick in Puddleglum in *The Silver Chair*, in MacPhee in *That Hideous Strength*, and in Digory (Professor *Kirke*).

As a result of all this, Lewis ranks among the great literary critics. And he notes a problem with Cicero: "The Two Great Bores (Demosthenes and Cicero) could not be avoided."[7] He had a great measure of romantic protection: "But this slight error saved me from that far deeper error of 'classicism' with which the Humanists have hoodwinked half the world."[8]

It was an imaginative book that undid Lewis and set him on the road to conversion. "Turning to the bookstall, I picked out an Everyman in a dirty jacket."[9] The book was *Phantastes* by George MacDonald. In his turn, Lewis has been used in the same way in the conversion of countless others. If we understand his "project," we will seek to write in a way that passes that opportunity on. He cites Chesterton as apropos: "The sword glitters not because the swordsman set out to make it glitter but because he is fighting for his life and therefore moving it very quickly."[10]

The medieval mind, which we must understand if we want to understand Lewis, was one that represented a literate culture that had somehow lost most of its books. Consequently, they had to make do with what few books they had. This meant that they were not quick to set their books at odds with one another. In addition to this, the temperament of the medieval man was one of organization. What the universe needed was a little tidying up. This means that they were great systematizers, great harmonizers. Sometimes the facts suffered a bit, but what is that among friends?

If you ever want to introduce someone to this perspective, in Lewis's words, and you don't think he would wade through *The Discarded Image*, there is a short essay that Lewis wrote that does the same work in a much briefer compass:

> I assume that everyone knows, more or less, its material layout: a motionless earth at the centre, transparent spheres revolving round it, of which the lowest, slowest, nearest and smallest carries the Moon, and thence upwards in the order Mercury, Venus, the Sun, Mars, Jupiter, Saturn; beyond these, all the stars in one sphere; beyond that, a sphere which carries no light but

merely imparts movement to those below it; beyond that, the Empyrean, the boundary of the *mundus*, the beginning of the infinite true "Heaven."[11]

Go out on any starry night and walk alone for half an hour, resolutely assuming that the pre-Copernican astronomy is true. Look up at the sky with that assumption in your mind. The real difference between living in that universe and living in ours will then, I predict, begin to dawn on you.[12]

You will be looking at a universe immense but finite. In this finite universe, the word *small* (as applied to earth) has meaning. In an infinite universe, small and large are equally meaningless. Infinity was, for the ancients, an incoherent concept. You will be considering the aspect of *height*. And you would be looking at something that was structured, built, or assembled.

We have real trouble giving the medievals a fair shake on this whole cosmological question. First, we insist that they are claiming things they never would claim, because that is what *we* might want to assert in similar circumstances. For example, we think the center is the most important thing, and so when we find out that they were geocentric, we think that they were making grandiose claims for themselves, when the precise opposite was true. The earth was the center of the cosmos, true enough, but this was not a statement of its importance. This was a lowly position. Think for a minute. If the earth was the center, what was at the very center of the earth in Dante's *Inferno*? Right—the Devil's hairy haunches, in the middle of hell.

Another grand error we make is that we mistake description for explanation, a mistake you would never find them making. What is gravity? What holds protons together? As Ramandu put it, "Even in your world, my son, that is not what a star is, but only what it is made of."[13]

Medieval man did not think that everything moved in obedience to impersonal laws, like the law of gravity. Rather, he felt that everything had its natural station and sought to get there. Many of the things that we today regard as inanimate were considered by them to be intelligent creatures. These creatures were busy loving God and trying to find the best place from which that love could be expressed. With regard to the planetary spheres, they moved in accordance with love. God, the immutable one, could not change. So how could such a creature imitate this perfect God? The closest imitative approach would be to travel in a perfect figure, i.e., a circle. A circle was perfect, everything in heaven was perfect, and so why should you look through a telescope?

Keep in mind that the battle between Galileo and the church was *not* a battle between science and mindless fundamentalism. It was a battle between new science and old science, and the error of the church had been that of getting into bed with the best science of the day. And we all know, as Max Planck put it, science advances funeral by funeral.

As Ovid put it, it is art to conceal art. *Ars est celere artem.* And as Lewis put it in a letter to Arthur Greeves, "As is proper in romance, the inner meaning is *carefully hidden*."[14] For many people (I am afraid Tolkien was among them), the images and symbols of the Narnia stories are a perfect hodgepodge, slapped together by a genius who couldn't be bothered to take any trouble over it. But still, despite this, the Narnia stories continue to have a mysterious power.

It is almost as though the engine that makes them go is invisible to us—until now. Michael Ward, the man who solved this riddle in *Planet Narnia*, deserves our deepest thanks. I have been steeped in the Narnia stories since I was a small boy and have written a book on what I learned there. In the acknowledgments of that book, I said, "It seems in retrospect that I was brought up as a Narnian. I am tempted to wonder why I don't need a green card to live here."[15] But precisely because of this, my astonishment in reading what Ward uncovered was beyond measure. I don't think it is really possible to understand Lewis's project without understanding Ward—and I think it is essential to understand Lewis.

What Lewis talked about in literary criticism of other books should be remembered when we come to consider *his* works of fiction. "Again and again, in defending works of romance, Lewis argues that it is the quality or tone of the whole story that is its main attraction."[16] But in order for this to work, it cannot be overtly flagged by the author.[17]

Those who have read *The Discarded Image* know the pleasure and affection that Lewis had for the medieval cosmology. He was steeped in this view and advanced many aspects of it unabashedly in the space trilogy (not to mention other places). Why should we think it incredible that he did something more surreptitiously in the Chronicles? Let us work through this not in chronological order or the order in which they were written, but let us ascend through the spheres.

In fiction, characters are described as flat or round—two-dimensional, or you feel like you know them as well as some of your friends. In Narnia, the backdrop, the atmosphere, is round, not flat. Why? Narnia is what it is and has the effect that it does because of its *donegality*. Ward picks up this word from a use in passing that Lewis gave it and defined it this way:

> By donegality we mean to denote the spiritual essence or quid-dity of a work of art as intended by the artist and inhabited unconsciously by the reader. The donegality of a story is its peculiar and deliberated atmosphere or quality; its pervasive and purposed integral tone or flavour; its tutelary by tacit spirit, a spirit that the author consciously sought to conjure, but which was designed to remain implicit in the matter of the text, despite being also concentrated and consummated in a Christologically representative character, the more influentially to inform the work and so affect the reader.[18]

If a decorator of a restaurant threw up a few things here and there for the sake of "atmosphere," the effect would be trivial. Atmosphere done right runs a lot deeper than that, and deep atmosphere in a work of literature is what we mean by donegality. So, do you know what Narnian air tastes like? And if you know, how did it come about that you know? Was it an accident? The first effect of the moon in *The Silver Chair* is that of wateriness. From beginning to end, the characters are wet, damp, soaked, teary, and so forth. Puddleglum is a watery creature with a watery name. Then there is the instability of those who are "moonstruck." Rilian wanders, looking for the murderer of his mother. The children wander in looking for him, because they gave off reciting the signs. Rilian is literally out of his mind during the hours when he is not strapped in the chair. Consider also the presence of "pale" throughout the book, the way you would look in the light of the moon. More positively, silver is the color of the moon, and from the silver chair itself, and from there on down, we see the color *silver* everywhere.

Gemini is ruled by Mercury, and the Gemini twins are Castor and Pollux. Castor is known as a breaker of horses (and Shasta is the horse-boy) and Pollux was a renowned boxer—just like Corin. This shows up repeatedly and is no accident. Throughout *The Horse and His Boy* twins and doubles are common, again, beyond the possibility of accident. Mercury has wings on his feet, and the basic thrust of this storyline is Shasta getting to Archenland in time in order to deliver his message. Mercury (or Hermes) is also the god of thieves, and Shasta has to do a bit of pilfering along the way. And in this book we see the importance of story as well as the importance of story moving from drab to glorious. The celebrations and stories at the end of this book are all anointed by Mercury.

A spirit of levity and mirth is pervasive in *The Magician's Nephew*. From the first joke of the jackdaw to the crowds in London laughing at Jadis, there is plenty of laughter. Jadis is Venus Infernal and is modeled after the Babylonian Venus (Ishtar) and in the book is, like Venus, dazzlingly beautiful. The point is emphasized again and again. The fertility of the earth at the creation by Aslan is a venereal theme. Digory swears *by gum* repeatedly in *Nephew*, and it is not coincidence. He is swearing by Venus, by her aromatic resins. And let us not forget the garden where Digory fetches the apple, an enclosed garden like the garden of the Hesperides.

The donegality of *The Voyage of the Dawn Treader* is, as Ward notes, the most obvious of all the Narniad. The book is all about the sun, sailing toward the sun. The metal that radiates from the sun is, of course, gold. We have the encounter with gold on Deathwater Island. The influence of Sol is that of making men generous, liberal. That is a theme throughout, even as early as Caspian's liberation of the Lone Islands. And Aslan appears numerous times in this book, each time becoming increasingly "solar."

Prince Caspian is a militant and martial book. No surprise there. Ward notes the two main themes coming from Mars—militarism and silvanism. We have a usurper king, a rebel army, forced marches, desperate flights, and single combat. And this is Mars Silvanus— woods are everywhere. The English kids land in the woods, woods grow up around the castle, they have to march through the woods, the Silvans come to fight against Miraz, and near the end of the book the woods successfully freak out the Telmarines.

Lewis says the "Jovial character is cheerful, festive, yet temperate, tranquil, magnanimous."[19] Those characteristics are pervasive throughout *The Lion, the Witch and the Wardrobe*, and (in the first book published) strike the keynote for the whole series, which was in fact the keynote of Lewis's temperament. He was, by design and by grace, a jovial man. *Lion* is about the passing of winter, an event that Lewis repeatedly elsewhere ties to the rule of Jove. We see "winter passed" (in Lewis's poem "The Planets"), and he uses the phrase "winter overgone" in *The Allegory of Love*. What character is more jovial than Father Christmas? And what better figure to illustrate how Lewis is creating the atmosphere he wants and needs, even if by means of characters that don't really belong. Notice that *Christmas* is in Narnia. The curse is lifted from Narnia, and it is no longer "always winter and never Christmas." Christmas doesn't belong in Narnia as a piece of furniture there, but it is not a piece of furniture. It is how the house is being defined. Also, Jove is royal—and the kingliness of Aslan is pronounced in *Lion*.

Lewis was jovial, not saturnine, but, as Ward says, he was fully prepared to give Saturn his due. *The Last Battle*, the first part of which is the grimmest part of the Narniad, is all about Saturn. In *The Silver Chair*, Father Time in the underworld was, in the earlier draft of the book, named as Saturn. Lewis removed it, presumably for the sake of keeping the planetary themes less visible. And Saturn stands up at the end of the world and puts out the sun. Everything about the story, until the death of Tirian, is grim and gray. Shift is from Saturn, as are the tragic events that culminate in Narnia's end. But then, in the last part of the book, Saturn gives way to Jove.

Owen Barfield once said that what Lewis thought about everything was contained in what he said about anything. This is why we find—in everything he wrote—passages or connections to everything else he wrote. Another way of putting it is, while Lewis wrote one book with *Wardrobe* in the title, every book he ever wrote had a wardrobe in it somewhere. There is a way to get to any of his books from any one of his books. He was an integrated personality who wrote books equally integrated.

Lewis says that *The Abolition of Man* addresses in nonfiction form the ideas that he presented in fictional guise in *That Hideous Strength*. The lectures out of which *Abolition* came were presented near Durham in the early part of 1943—roughly around the time of the battle at Stalingrad. We are still over a year away from Normandy. *That Hideous Strength* came out the year the war ended, meaning that Lewis was working on it during the war. The essay "The Poison of Subjectivism," mentioned earlier, published in *Christian Reflections*, is an article-length version of the central thoughts in *Abolition*.

What kind of education system produced the flaccid Mark Studdock? To ask the question is to call to mind the education system that Lewis declared war on in this book. *The Abolition of Man* is a book about education and about the subtlety of propaganda. At the same time, there is nothing subtle about its destructive results and consequences. "I doubt whether we are sufficiently attentive to the importance of elementary textbooks."[20]

Lewis is greatly concerned here with how the process of education is capable of destroying children and, through them, of destroying great civilizations. The thing that set Lewis off was the very clever inculcation of subjectivism. In the story about the waterfall, the authors of the text said that to say that something is sublime is really only to say that I have certain feelings that can be associated with the word *sublime*. And when this lesson is mastered, all of Western civilization falls. "The authors themselves, I suspect, hardly know what they are doing to the boy, and he cannot know what is being done to him."[21]

Lewis is at war with the insidiousness of subjectivism:

> The human mind has no more power of inventing a new value than of planting a new sun in the sky or a new primary colour in the spectrum. . . . Every attempt to do so consists in arbitrarily selecting some one maxim of traditional morality, isolating it from the rest, and erecting it into an *unum necessarium*.[22]

You have all the characters of Belbury on the one hand, and the defenseless pawns, like Mark Studdock, on the other. Consider this:

> [A mawkish appeal] falls equally flat on those who are above it and those who are below it, on the man of real sensibility and on the mere trousered ape who has never been able to conceive the Atlantic as anything more than so many million tons of cold salt water.[23]

What happens then?

> The task of the modern educator is not to cut down jungles but to irrigate deserts. The right defense against false sentiments is to inculcate just sentiments. By starving the sensibility of our pupils we only make them easier prey to the propagandist when

he comes. For famished nature will be avenged and a hard heart is no infallible protection against a soft head.[24]

When we are done with this kind of education, we will often be shocked at the success of our efforts. "In a sort of ghastly simplicity" men without chests are in the process of ceasing to be, if you will, "talking beasts."

Lewis was an imaginative genius. But more than that, he was a man who understood that a rightly ordered imagination was a fortress for the rational capacities of man. It is not the way we normally suppose. It is easy to think that clearheadedness is the fortress and that it protects the imagination, what we are allowed to play with in our recreational hours. But Lewis's tough-mindedness was the result of having been given a sanctified imagination. In the apostle Paul we see the same kind of thing—it is the peace of God that passes understanding that protects our "hearts and . . . minds" (Phil. 4:7). It is not the other way around. One of the reasons many apologists are not nearly as effective as Lewis is that they want the cold granite of reason to do everything. But true reason will collapse before a false imagination. False imagination must be answered by a true imagination, and when that happens, reason can flourish in its native habitat.

Because he was steeped in the right kind of story, Lewis was particularly good on the mushiness of subjectivism. The issues surrounding the objectivity of morality are never going to go out of style.

> Either the maxims of traditional morality must be accepted as axioms of practical reason which neither admit nor require argument to support them and not to "see" which is to have lost human status; or else there are no values at all, what we mistook for values being "projections" or irrational emotions.[25]

IF YOU READ NOTHING ELSE

Most people know Lewis through Narnia, and if you have not read these seven books, I urge you to start there. Since most people reading this book will likely have read the Narniad repeatedly, I would recommend here something I haven't done in the other chapters. I would strongly urge lovers of Narnia to read Michael Ward's *Planet Narnia*. If time is an issue, Ward has a shorter version of the same thesis, written on a more popular level—*The Narnia Code*. I grew up in Narnia, and have always loved it there, and have read the books again and over again, but Ward really took me further up and further in.

Lewis's fictional trilogy should be read—*Out of the Silent Planet*; *Perelandra*; and *That Hideous Strength*. All of them should be read at least once, and I recommend that readers return to *That Hideous Strength* again and again. I believe it to have been one of the great novels of the twentieth century—wise and prophetic.

When it comes to his popular theological work, I will mention just a few and work manfully to restrain myself. Read *Mere Christianity*; *The Abolition of Man*; *The Screwtape Letters*; *The Great Divorce*; *God in the Dock*; *The Weight of Glory* . . . oh, I give up. If you would like to read something of his professional work, I recommend *The Discarded Image*.

Of course, all his work is valuable, and by recommending these, I wouldn't want anyone to think I was urging him to stop there.

R. F. Capon

A WRITER'S LIFE

Robert Farrar Capon was born in Queens, New York, in 1925, and went to meet his Lord in 2013. He ministered for more than fifty years as an Episcopal parish priest on Long Island. For twenty-seven years he was dean of the seminary in Garden City, New York, a professor of theology, a canon theologian to the bishop of Long Island, a teacher of cooking, and a freelance food writer for the *New York Times*, *Newsday*, and many magazines. A nationally known lecturer, he was enthusiastically received by numerous audiences over the course of many years. It was in 1977 that he gave himself more fully to writing, cooking, and lecturing. But, of course, there is more to his story than that.

In his preface to *The Romance of the Word*, Capon gives us something of an autobiographical overview, and much of what follows is taken from there. *The Romance of the Word* is an assemblage of three of Capon's early books, and in the preface, written many years later, he describes his personal and theological pilgrimage, as woven together with all his books.

I should perhaps begin by saying I appreciated the fact that he anticipated something that contributed to my selection of most of the authors I am treating in this book: "The authors of whom I have made great use are C. S. Lewis, G. K. Chesterton, T. S. Eliot,

W. H. Auden, and, just to prove I'm not hung up on Englishmen with two initials, Matthew, Mark, Luke and John."[1] I proved *my* freedom from that same hang-up by not talking about Auden at all and by including four Americans, including Capon. Not only that, but I cheated on the initials with two of them, including Capon.

His first book, *Bed and Board*, was published in 1965, and it became a best seller. It was, as he put it, "a celebration of my own peculiar marriage."[2] Despite feeling a bit apologetic for the overly masculine feel of that book, showing that decades in a mainline denomination will take its toll even on the crustiest of curmudgeons, years later he still thought the book stood up well. He marked with gratitude the fact that he had been allowed to "embark on the leaky love boat of marital life" with that book.[3] But, he points out, mark that word *leaky*:

> Thirty years after *Bed and Board*, I am divorced from Margaret and at varying distances from my long-since grown children. As it has turned out, there were a lot of departments in which I was not a success, not to mention several in which I was, and still am, a failure. Even such successes as I had were absurdly different from anything I had in mind. I dedicated a great deal of time and effort to my children's religious formation, only to find them now mostly uninterested and non-practicing.[4]

At the same time, he says, he threw himself into cooking in order to please only himself, and the result was that he produced "a whole family of good cooks and happy omnivores."[5] Ain't it the way, he mutters.

> After twenty-seven years of marriage to Margaret, I asked for a divorce and married my wife Valerie, acquiring two more children, Laura and Erik, in the bargain. At the time, the bishop took a dim view of my plans.[6]

This "dim view" that the bishop had taken about his plans to divorce and remarry meant that Capon lost his two jobs with the church, since those two jobs were dependent upon the bishop. Capon had been dean of the diocesan seminary, and he had been the priest-in-charge of a mission church. The bishop gave Capon the option of resigning to avoid the sack, and so he took his severance pay and went off to support himself as a freelance writer.

I was not deposed or suspended from the priesthood, so I still continued to function as an occasional Sunday-supply priest; but for a number of years, Valerie's and my income consisted almost entirely of what I could earn by my food-writing wits.[7]

Eventually he was hired, for twelve years, as an assistant at St. Luke's Church in East Hampton, New York, and then worked five more years as an interim priest at Christ Church in Greenport, New York.

Two of his early books had sold quite well, while the others, to use his phrase, "sold like coldcakes." *Bed and Board* was a best seller, as was *The Supper of the Lamb* a few years later (1969). As a result he could still get books into print but usually not with significant advances. Writing theological books of that sort is not hand to mouth, but rather mouth to hand:

What saved us back then was writing numerous articles of food for *The New York Times, Newsday, Redbook, Working Mother, Connoisseur, Eating Well,* and other publications.[8]

So the result of all this was a renegade priest in good standing, theologically trained, producing his brand of theology and cookbooks, and gathering a very eclectic herd of followers. Conservatives love him for this, and liberals love him for that, and a bunch of people aren't sure why they love him. But something clicks.

Near the end of his life, he suffered from hydrocephalus. Though he still had his wits about him (he mostly had trouble walking), he wasn't up for visits from his fans. He celebrated Holy Communion every day with Valerie, translating from the Greek Scriptures as they did so. But his days for being interviewed were over. He said that all he ever wanted to say about theology could be found between the covers of his books. The answers to the questions anyone might have were already there.

He died September 5, 2013, year of our Lord.

DIGGING DEEPER

For sheer exuberance in writing, Robert Farrar Capon had few who could keep up with him. In the great cross-country race for the colorful metaphor, he was the kind of runner who could climb trees during the race to allow the other runners time to catch up. I would have said the "trees of hyperbole," but that would have been pushing it, even for me.

I want to argue (now briefly, later at greater length) that there is a deep connection between a grasp of the unmerited grace of God and colorful writing. Here is Capon, making the foundation of this point:

> The Reformation was a time when men went blind, staggering drunk because they had discovered, in the dusty basement of late medievalism, a whole cellar full of fifteen-hundred-year-old, two-hundred proof Grace—bottle after bottle of pure distillate of Scripture, one sip of which would convince anyone that God saves us single-handedly.[9]

Now I grant that nothing is very tidy in this world, a datum that Capon was most capable of pointing out. He excelled in pointing it out. In fact, Capon himself was one of those untidy data. He was so into grace that he is fully capable—in places—of sounding like Marcion after a couple of beers. But like Antole in Wodehouse, we must learn to take a few roughs with the smooth.

Here is Capon on how God created the world:

> So they shouted together "*Tov meod!*" and they laughed for ages and ages, saying things like how great it was for beings to be, and how clever of the Father to think of the idea, and how kind of the Son to go to all that trouble putting it together, and

how considerate of the Spirit to spend so much time directing and choreographing. And for ever and ever they told old jokes, and the Father and the Son drank their wine *in unitate Spiritus Sancti*, and they all threw ripe olives and pickled mushrooms at each other *per omnia saecula saeculorum*, Amen.

It is, I grant you, a crass analogy; but crass analogies are the safest. Everybody knows that God is not three old men throwing olives at each other. Not everyone, I'm afraid, is equally clear that God is not a cosmic force or a principle of being or any other dish of celestial blancmange we might choose to call him. Accordingly, I give you the central truth that creation is the result of a trinitarian bash, and leave the details of the analogy to sort themselves out as best they can.[10]

The point is much larger than Capon and every bit as messy.

Wycliffe is called the Morning Star of the Reformation, but I think we need to start calling Chaucer the poet laureate of that great gloaming of grace. John of Gaunt was the patron of both men, and there are good reasons for understanding Chaucer as among, or sympathetic to, the Lollards—the followers of Wycliffe. This makes some of our virginal librarians nervous, because of "The Miller's Tale" and such like, but Chaucer himself published a postscript that said *heh, heh, went a little far sometimes*. When the wineskins burst, grace sometimes gets on the floor. That is why the grace of God even gives us cleanup crews—we need the virginal librarians too. Like Lucy, I wouldn't feel safe around Bacchus unless Aslan were near.

Find me a place where grace has gone and taken deep root, and I will show you a place where vivid prose flourishes. We find a man like Tyndale at the headwaters of the obvious, and the Elizabethan supernova came from somewhere. For the most rambunctious specimen from that era, I would offer up Martin Marprelate, the man who gave us the immortal line of the bishops who had "learnt their catechisms and were past grace."

And scholar Peter Escalante has done some excellent work on the Italian humanists, who predated the Reformation, but who contributed mightily to it. His work on this sets out a tantalizing set of clues to pursue along these lines. What I need to do, actually, is learn how to read faster.

Napoleon once said that imagination rules the world. That is very true, but we need to add something to that. We must choose between the corrupted imagination, the escapist imagination, the despairing imagination, and—here it comes—the *forgiven* imagination.

But where are the brakes on this thing? Are brakes needed?

> I have for a long time now been on two major theological kicks: an uncompromising insistence on grace alone through faith as God's way of dealing with the world, and a perpetual harping on the fact that Christianity is not a religion.[11]

Now Capon is not a universalist, but there is a reason he had to answer questions about it all the time. He believes that hell is a reality in the text that cannot be avoided. But he absolutizes grace and forgiveness in a particular way and holds that the most sunken sinner in the deepest pit of that hell is a person who is entirely and completely *forgiven*, and that the only barrier to his enjoyment of salvation is his own perverse choices. In other words, grace is what it is regardless of what the recipient thinks about it or does with it. Religion—that which Christianity is not—for Capon is a tangle of bookkeeping transactions, and because of his view of absolute grace, there is no transaction involved.

Now we have to agree that grace, being a sheer gift of the inexhaustible God, cannot really be overdone. But it can be misunderstood, and however much we exult in Capon's gift for expressing himself on the subject of grace, we do need to reel it in a bit. We cannot reel in the actual grace of God—let it run, as though we had a choice—but it is pretty important for us to reel in some of Capon's peculiar understandings of grace.

No one can read any long document (other than a lease or a will) without having to decide which of its insistences or stipulations he or she thinks central and which peripheral. And therefore no careful readers of Scripture—not even those (such as myself) who hold it to be the Word of God—can dispense themselves from the necessity of putting the arm on the peripheral in favor of the central.[12]

He is quite right in saying that certain things in the Bible are more important than other things. Jesus tells us that some commandments are greater than others, for example (Matt. 22:38–40). And Paul tells us that certain parts of his teaching were much more important than other parts (1 Cor. 15:3). This is quite different from saying that certain themes in Scripture are important and true and other elements are not as important, and wrong to boot.

Paul, when he speaks to the responsible heirs of the Jewish tradition, is full of grace, freedom, and forgiveness; but when he writes to Greeks whose sexual mores, for example, make his pharisaic flesh creep, he sounds exactly like an Old Testament Jewish uncle.[13]

In other words, Paul sounds exactly like Capon wants us to quit sounding when confronted with a twenty-first-century version of what used to set Paul off. To Capon's credit, he doesn't try to pretend that Paul didn't say such things. But he does get dangerously close to "don't try this at home." Paul gets a pass, but we do not.

The problem with this approach—that of reading any long document that is not a will or a lease—and pulling out all the grace bits in order to chortle over them, and leaving in the chaff of law and works so that a celestial janitor can sweep them away later, is that it precludes any true harmonization of them. But if the law is grace, and if grace has a backbone, perhaps we ought not be too dismissive of those who have learned how to hold the Word of God in both hands.

Capon was very exuberant and colorful as he did it, but it must be admitted that he was a cherry picker. And the problem is not the cherries he gets; the problem is how easy it is for him to disparage anything he didn't pick himself. And he has a tendency to say that the cherries at the top of the tree aren't cherries at all.

> The predestinarian buffs, of course, got it right: people don't work themselves into salvation; God puts them there by his own inscrutable will. But the predestinarians blew it when they decided that God also put a whole bunch of people outside the reconciliation—just because he felt like it. They passed the course entitled Unmerited Grace 309 with flying colors; but they flunked Catholicity 101.[14]

Here is the difficulty. The "buffs," as he describes them, are not just people with pinched faces trying to work out their personality disorders. Rather, they are many committed Christians and faithful exegetes—as liberated and full of grace as Capon might be able to describe on a particularly ebullient morning—who want to be faithful to the *entire* text of Scripture. But Capon prefers to pick and choose, and when he celebrates what he has picked, there are few who can do it better. But what he left behind should be celebrated also and really needs to be.

We should find someone with Capon's verbal gifts and ask him to describe how the law of the Lord is perfect, converting the soul. We need someone who can successfully compare a theonomic ethic with mayo, onions, and melted cheese, open-faced, on a piece of toast done just right. That, and a good book and an open fire in the next room. It could even be one of Greg Bahnsen's books.

> All of the raw materials for double predestination—for God's right to condemn whoever he damn well pleases—come pouring out of him [Paul]; the pot that can't speak back to the potter, the potter who is free to make vases of chamberpots, and so on. The dreadful doctrine of divine reprobation, there, is based on a misreading—not, admittedly, of Paul's actual words, for he did indeed say all those hard things, but *of the force of his words in the context of his whole argument.*[15]

This approach forces Capon into an unfortunate double standard. When Paul says various contradictory things, he is given a pass. But when *we* repeat Paul's hard words, seeking to place them in the same context that Paul did, we find ourselves described as the elder brother in the parable of the prodigal son: "tub-thumpers for a hard-line God."[16]

In other words, when Paul does it, his words are placed in their appropriate context because he so clearly gets "the grace thing" in other passages. But when other people try it, they find that they have flunked Catholicity 101. The problem is that—on Capon's terms—Paul did more poorly in that class than even we are doing. "If anyone has no love for the Lord, let him be accursed. Our Lord, come!" (1 Cor. 16:22).

But Capon had a gift, and in certain key areas, he was a gift. One blessing Capon has for us is found in his liberation from every form of food pharisaism. He was a fine cook and a fine observer of what went on the table and what went into getting it there. *Bed and Board* started out as a cookbook that got diverted into a book on marriage. And Capon's central contribution to our mental health was *The Supper of the Lamb*, a book that is simply wonderful. If there is any place where Capon's antinomianism is likely to be a great help to us all, it would be in what he has to say about all the food fussers. This is not an irrelevant concern, for when it comes to food fussing, we are a wicked and adulterous generation. In this regard we would take the cake except we are afraid it might have gluten in it.

> My own feeling, however, is that they need something else even more. They need to have their tastes *un*balanced: to have them skewed, driven off dead center, and fastened firmly to the astonishing oddness of the world.[17]

I used the word *antinomian* positively here, and this is because on the matter of food, the teaching of Scripture is *that there is no law*. Where God has given no law, an occasional visit from the rowdy antinomians might prove useful.

Nothing is plainer in the New Testament than that God doesn't care what we eat. He cares how we eat, and he cares with whom we eat. But it is a matter of spiritual indifference as to what we put in our mouths. Note that I used the word *spiritual* there. If your child is allergic to peanuts, and eating one will cause the entire family to spend a worried evening praying down at the ER, then, sure, in that sense, God cares what you eat. But God does not care what we eat in the way that food fussers believe he does:

> "Do you not see that whatever goes into a person from outside cannot defile him, since it enters not his heart but his stomach, and is expelled?" (Thus he declared all foods clean). (Mark 7:18–19)

> If with Christ you died to the elemental spirits of the world, why, as if you were still alive in the world, do you submit to regulations—"Do not handle, Do not taste, Do not touch." (Col. 2:20–21)

> As for the one who is weak in faith, welcome him, but not to quarrel over opinions. One person believes he may eat anything, while the weak person eats only vegetables. (Rom. 14:1–2)

Capon in the kitchen actually provides just the right blend of law surrounded by grace; he actually does far better on this task in the kitchen than he does in theology proper.

On the one hand, he is a man of standards. His tastes are highly refined and disciplined. He knows what needs to go into a meal. He knows how to express himself freely when it comes to certain edible outrages—"supermarket Swiss (which has the texture, but nowhere near the flavor, of rubber gloves)."[18] "Any man who cannot tell the difference between butter and margarine has callouses on the inside of his mouth."[19] He has opinions. He cares about how we do food. And, were he still here, I am sure he would say with a sneer that we do not "do" food, but rather *eat* it and wash it down with the things that we *drink*. Having accepted this correction, I simply note that Capon believes that issues of eternal moment are worked out in the kitchen. It is one of the key places for us to work out our salvation with fear and trembling. As Teresa of Avila put it, "God walks among the pots and pans."

> A woman with her sleeves rolled up and flour on her hands is one of the most gorgeous stabilities in the world.[20]

But then Capon surprises us. One of the great problems with developed sensibilities in any area is the temptation to preciosity. Overrefinement in art, music, language, or any area does not create the true *artiste* but rather the insufferable boor. The task is not to cultivate high standards; any lout can do that. The trick is to cultivate high standards without turning into the person that every normal person in the world wants to avoid. And Capon achieves this gloriously. He is disciplined, focused, and all about food, without putting on airs. There is nothing of the culinary snob about him.

> On the other hand, I am wild about peanut butter and canned fruit cocktail (even the kind that tastes like the can). I will eat as much process cheese as I am handed, and I have been known to put mayonnaise on cooked pears.[21]

Little asides like this from him are not offered as confessions of his surreptitious and guilty pleasures, for there appears to be no sense of guilt at all. But he does not eat "low" because he has no awareness of what he is doing, like the fellow who has only ten taste buds for every square inch of his tongue and struggles to determine the difference between hot and cold. No, Capon is given over to his fascination with food. The second chapter of *The Supper of the Lamb* is an extended meditation on an onion, a noble creature that was able to make Capon exult under the wild creativity of God:

> Drive far from us, O Most Bountiful, all creatures of air and darkness; cast out the demons that possess us; deliver us from the fear of calories and the bondage of nutrition; and set us free once more in our own land, where we shall serve thee as

thou hast blessed us—with the dew of heaven, the fatness of the earth, and plenty of corn and wine. Amen.[22]

We were given every tree in the garden to eat, all but one, and so we should set about the business of eating the world. We should resist, as dangerous false doctrine, the idea that we should line up a list of restrictions for the palate.

No, again: we are omnivores; we have bodies specifically designed to digest such things, if they are taken in moderation. But alas, moderation is not nearly as much our cup of tea as religion is; so we learn our food catechism (even though it's revised every few months by the high priests of health), we keep the food commandments as if our life depended on them—and then we wonder why, if we are all such good boys and girls, our meals look and taste like prison fare.[23]

In short, Capon knows what food is *for*. Food is for fellowship. Food requires sauces so that it can serve as a brown-gravy parable; this is because all food, of every comestible kind, is the sauce for the true food of true fellowship.

The central point of the food is not what you are eating but rather who you are eating it with—but don't mistake the point here. That does not make the taste of the food, or the care that goes into its preparation, irrelevant. Far from it. A good sauce accents the taste of the food, and good cooking accents the taste of the fellowship. Capon knows that the real point of food is *companionship*—a word that comes from the Latin word for bread, *panis*. We treat the bread as important because the companion is important. And we should treat our food with exuberance because we want to adorn the food of communion.

But this requires a certain attitude, and we practice that attitude as we mess around with our sauces.

There is almost no sauce that will not be improved by having a lump of butter whisked into it the moment before it is served. . . . Dishes should come to the table vested, robed. . . . A great sauce deserves a great finish. Whatever you do, therefore, don't omit the final grace—the loving pat of butter.[24]

The true food at table is the saying of grace, the song, the jokes, the laughter, the stories from the day, the passing of the cheese potatoes along with a wink and a nudge to indicate that you share the recipient's opinion of them, which is high.

To be sure, food keeps us alive, but that is only its smallest and most temporary work. Its *eternal* purpose is to furnish our sensibilities against the day when we shall sit down at the heavenly banquet and see how gracious the Lord is. Nourishment is necessary only for a while; what we shall need forever is *taste*.[25]

One of the impulses that overscrupulous pietists have is that of trying to "thin out the world" so that we won't be as tempted to idolatry by it. But the problem with this procedure is that it never works. We can fall into idolatry with our airy abstractions as much as we do with a gold-plated statue of Buddha with baskets of fruit in front of it.

We need to see God on the other side of the world; we need to adore him through what he has given us and because he has given it to us. But to do this rightly, we have to see the world as *thicker* than we normally do. Pouring a gallon of a pungent solvent into our bucket of worldly goods will not make us any less attached to our own idolatrous whimsies. This is especially the case if our idolatrous whimsy consists of trying to thin out the world God created. Who do we think we are?

G. K. Chesterton sees the world as thicker than most men do, and yet he is plainly free of the wrong kinds of attachments to it. In *Pied Beauty*, Gerard Manley Hopkins makes us truly see the glory of God in earthy things. The poem begins with "Glory be to God" and concludes with "praise him." But we would not increase God's glory in the poem if we had poured our solvent all over it.

Glory be to God for barely visible things,
For skies kind of bland, and not show-offy.

No. We must never despise the Giver because we have been
distracted by the gift. Some have done this, but this is never fixed
by wrecking the gift. Picture our various theologies of this folly on
Christmas morning. If you open a gift and churlishly refuse to thank
the giver of it, then—in our little illustration—you are an atheist.
But how, in this regard, is it better to be the pietist and to smash
the gift to pieces "lest it tempt you away from your devotion to the
giver"? I can pretty much guarantee that such pietism would not
fly if I tried it on my wife. She would say, in that sensible way of
hers, that smashing gifts is not the best way of showing gratitude.

And this brings us back to Capon.

> The world is no disposable ladder to heaven. Earth is not con-
> venient, it is good; it is, by God's design, our lawful love.[26]

Capon is at war with ethereal gnosticism in all its forms:

> May your table be graced with lovely women and good men.
> May you drink well enough to drown the envy of youth in the
> satisfactions of maturity. May your men wear their weight with
> pride, secure in the knowledge that they have become consid-
> erable. . . . May there be singing at our table before the night
> is done, and old broad jokes to fling at the stars and tell them
> that we are men. . . . The road to Heaven does not run *from* the
> world but *through* it.[27]

IF YOU READ NOTHING ELSE

The one book you must read by Capon, if you read no other, is *The
Supper of the Lamb* (1969). In it, his love of creation straight up
is on full display. Not only does he love the created order; he is a
careful and close observer of it. He *notices* things. (As already mentioned, take, for example, his description of an onion in this book.)

His first book was *Bed and Board*, which was published in

1965. This, together with *Supper*, sold better than his others, and if you proceed on the assumption that they did so for a reason, you could do worse than to simply read these two.

If you want a taste of his exegetical and theological writing, I recommend his trilogy on the parables of Jesus: *The Parables of Grace*; *The Parables of the Kingdom*; and *The Parables of Judgment*. Proceed with caution; he is frequently insightful and just as frequently erratic and unreliable. These are available in one volume called simply *Kingdom, Grace, Judgment*. There are just a handful of writers who can edify you while simultaneously exasperating you, but Capon is in that number. God bless him.

8

M. S. Robinson

A WRITER'S LIFE

Yes, despite the fact that Marilyn Robinson doesn't write under the name M. S. Robinson, I wanted to include her anyway, along with Robert Capon, and it was Emerson who taught us that a foolish consistency is the hobgoblin of little minds. The former archbishop of Canterbury, Rowan Williams, has praised her as among the world's "most compelling" novelists in the English language, but despite the high praise coming from that quarter, I thought it was important to honor Robinson's writing anyway.

Robinson was born in 1943 in Sandpoint, Idaho, which, as interested readers might want to note, is just up the road a piece from where I write these words.

As anyone who has read her novels will know, *place* is not just an arbitrary marking, a mere matter of latitude and longitude. She discussed her roots in the West in an essay called "When I Was a Child," but before getting to her discussion of the meaning of place, we might have to get a little provincialism out of the way:

> I went to college in New England and I have lived in Massachusetts for twenty years, and I find that the hardest work in the world—in fact it may be impossible—is to persuade Easterners that growing up in the West is not intellectually crippling. On

learning that I am from Idaho, people have not infrequently asked "Then how were you able to write a book?"[1]

As a fellow Idahoan, together with Robinson, the temptation occurs to me—and I resist it manfully *as* a temptation—to inquire into whether the provincial typhloticness, if that's a word, might be located in another region of the country entirely.

But despite her aboriginal geographic limitations, Robinson won the Pulitzer Prize for Fiction in 2005 for *Gilead* and was awarded the National Humanities Medal in 2013. Her first novel, *Housekeeping*, set in a fictional town here in north Idaho, was a finalist for the Pulitzer. It turns out she *can* write a book.

She is a quintessentially American writer: "I have spent most of my life studying American history and literature. I have studied other histories and literatures largely to gain perspective on this civilization. The magnanimity of its greatest laws and institutions as well as its finest poetry and philosophy move me very deeply."[2]

All but one of the writers addressed in this book are professing Christians of one stripe or another, H. L. Mencken being the one who opted out. Robinson was brought up as a Presbyterian, moving on to Congregationalism. This is mirrored by the close friendship of Broughton and Ames in *Gilead*—a Presbyterian minister and Congregational minister, respectively.

She described herself as shaped by the books she read when young; hence the title *When I Was a Child I Read Books*. She put it this way:

> The shelves of northern Idaho groaned with just the sort of old dull books I craved, so I cannot have been alone in these enthusiasms. Relevance was precisely not an issue for me. I looked to Galilee for meaning and to Spokane for orthodonture, and beyond that the world where I was I found entirely sufficient.[3]

She got her sense of rooted place from where she was, and she got her cosmopolitanism from the printed page.

When she left for college, she encountered a hard-core behavioral reductionism in her classes: "What Freud thought was important because it was Freud who thought it, and so with B. F. Skinner and whomever else the curriculum held up for our admiration."[4] But she was retrieved from the edge of that dismal swamp by means of a stray footnote in an odd book:

> And then my philosophy professor assigned us Jonathan Edwards's *Doctrine of Original Sin Defended*, in which Edwards argues for "the arbitrary constitution of the universe," illustrating his point with a gorgeous footnote about moonlight that even then began to dispel the dreary determinisms I was learning elsewhere. Improbable as that may sound to those who have not read the footnote.[5]

This is another characteristic feature of her thought, which we will discuss further in just a few pages, but this tendency appears to have begun early. She is no theological conservative, but she has a deep appreciation for a number of historical figures routinely lionized by conservatives—Edwards, Calvin, Tyndale, and so on. And she does this in a lively and intelligent interaction with those figures.

At the same time, Robinson is friendly to and part of what once were known as the mainstream denominations and occasionally preaches in the church where she worships. And so anyone who knows the conservative emphases that have characterized my own ministry over the years might wonder at her inclusion in this book. After a few moments of embarrassed throat clearing, the question comes. Isn't that kind of *liberal*? Sure, but H. L. Mencken was a flaming infidel, and I like him too. The reason for her inclusion here is quite simple—that woman can *write*.

DIGGING DEEPER

One of the verses that every novelist should internalize is this one: "The one who states his case first seems right, until the other comes and examines him" (Prov. 18:17). Everyone has a story, and everyone has a point, even if it is all messed up.

Flat characters move around in their novels like cardboard cut-outs on the top of a model train, with a herky-jerky motion. They might have motivations, but nobody understands them, least of all the author. Round characters are characters from which—if we may be permitted to speak this way—the author has heard their side of the story and has heard them out. This ability to empathize with her characters is one of the things that makes Robinson's novels so remarkable. She does it very well. Her characters stand out because she lets them stand up:

> For me, at least, writing consists very largely of exploring in-tuition. A character is really the sense of character, embodied, attired, and given voice as he or she seems to require. Where does this creature come from? From watching, I suppose. From reading emotional significance in gestures and inflections, as we all do all the time. These moments of intuitive recognition float free from their particular occasions and recombine them-selves into nonexistent people the writer and, if all goes well, the reader feel they know.[6]

A moment later, she adds this:

> When a writer knows *about* his character he is writing for plot. When he *knows* his character he is writing to explore, to feel reality on a set of nerves somehow not quite his own.[7]

This might seem like an odd place to bring in Stephen King, but I am afraid I am going to do it anyway. I have never read any of his novels and never intend to, but I will read virtually anything on the craft of wordsmithing, and Stephen King has one such book, called *On Writing*. In that book he writes about some of the kids he knew in high school that went into his character Carrie. He said this: "I never liked Carrie. . . . But through Sondra and Dodie I came at last to understand her a little. I pitied her and I pitied her classmates as well, because I had been one of them once upon a time."[8]

He didn't particularly like her, but at least he had heard her side of the story.

Robinson feels reality on sets of nerves not her own. This she highlights remarkably in her books *Gilead* and *Home*. In *Gilead* she writes in the first person, as an elderly pastor named John Ames. In *Home* she writes about the same basic set of characters and events but in the third person, from the perspective of the home of Broughton, John Ames's best friend.

Home is a cliffhanger and a nail-biter in which absolutely nothing happens. But Robinson does not resort to explosions, or intrigue, or motorcycle gangs rolling through in order to keep our interest. She doesn't need to. On top of that, *Home* is the same basic story told over again from another corner of the same little sleepy town. In other words, nothing happened *twice*. And yet both stories grip.

Neither book is written as a prequel or sequel but rather simultaneously, working through the same basic events from a different perspective entirely. This achieves a dramatic and striking effect, going back up to the point of Proverbs 18:17.

For example, in both books Jack Broughton, the prodigal son, screws up the courage to attend church to hear Ames preach. In *Gilead* he comes off to Ames as a sneering mocker but in *Home* as a devastated and broken man. Both perspectives make perfect sense in their respective contexts, which reminds us, yet again, that everyone has a set of controlling assumptions that set the tone of the narrative as they understand it.

Robinson is fond of all her characters, and it becomes impossible for the reader, over the course of the novel, not to share in that affection. She does have one blind spot in this regard, which we will discuss shortly, but in her novels, and in her discussion of historical events, she is about as evenhanded as it gets.

She can see and identify failings, but she is quick to contexualize them. Speaking of cultural development in America, she regularly says things like this: "We [Americans] learned early to live with diversity, *at least by the standards of the time.*"[9] After the Civil War, "the country came through it all at last, fairly intact by *the standards that apply in such cases.*"[10] "In terms of the time, as things go in this world, the policies that opened the West were sophisticated, considered, and benign."[11]

She is also quick to reject simplistic and isolated condemnations and equally quick to ask, *What are we actually comparing this to? What were the alternatives?* Robinson believes that "history is a dialectic of bad and worse,"[12] and she does not want to fall into the worse for the sake of avoiding the bad. If instead of the Mongol Invasion of Europe in the thirteenth century, we could simply have had free chocolate milk for everyone involved, that would have been much nicer. But it also wasn't one of the options. It kind of didn't happen.

What all this means is that a character found in one of Robinson's books can assume that he or she will enjoy the benevolence of a fair-minded author. This is a rare gift.

But she is not limited to characters and their motivations. Earlier, I mentioned Robinson's uncanny sense of place and her ability to capture the way the very air feels in that place. I see this firsthand in her novel *Housekeeping* because I live where this novel is set. Well, actually, it would be more accurate to say that I live *near* where it is set. The town is a fictional Fingerbone, Idaho, set next to one of the lakes we have here. There is no such place, and yet if you knew this region, you might expect to drive into it unexpectedly by taking a different route to Coeur d'Alene. It is clearly right around the next bend.

The lake itself amounts to a character in the novel, a dark, inscrutable, bottomless thing, and even *that* is true to the region. For example, Lake Pend Oreille, the lake right next to Sandpoint, where Robinson grew up, was deep enough for the Navy to use for a training submarine during the Second World War. The lake at Fingerbone was that kind of deep and foreboding lake.

Ruthie, the main character, had a grandfather who died in the lake; it was a train accident, where the train went off the bridge, and disappeared into the depths, like a fisherman dropping a length of cold chain into the water over the side of his rowboat. The train just slid to the bottom. "The disaster had fallen out of sight, like the train itself, and if the calm that followed it was not greater than the calm that came before it, it had seemed so."[13]

The lake just keeps coming back. Ruthie's mother had committed suicide by driving a borrowed car into the lake, which was how Ruthie and her sister Lucille had come to live there, first with their grandmother and then with their aunt.

One time when the lake was frozen, the snow in the hills melted, followed by rain. The town flooded. "The clashes and groans from the lake continued unabated, dreadful at night, and the sound of the night wind in the mountains was like one long indrawn breath."[14]

> Only the calm persistence with which the water touched, and touched, and touched, sifting all the little stones, jet, and white, and hazel, forced us to remember that the lake was vast, and in league with the moon (for no sublunar account could be made of its shimmering, cold life).[15]

The Inland Northwest is known as "big sky country": a lot of territory, and not very many people. I am fond of telling people that Moscow, where I live, has about twenty-two thousand people in it. With that number, it is the twelfth largest town in Idaho. We used to be the tenth largest, but we quit paying attention and slipped somehow. In Robinson's *Housekeeping*, there is a heavy sense of place, with space in every direction. Feel how this feels:

> The woods themselves disturbed us. . . . But the deep woods are as dark and stiff and as full of their own odors as the parlor of an old house. We would walk among those giant legs, hearing the enthralled and incessant murmurings far above our heads, like children at a funeral.[16]

These places in the deep woods are as quiet and solemn as a back room of an abandoned house. But this is not something that we should simply relegate to the realm of the creepy. No, something else is going on:

> A man in Alabama asked me how I felt the West was different from the East and the South, and I replied that in the West "lonesome" is a word with strong positive connotations.[17]

It is not possible to see society without the individual or the individual apart from society. But in these times, it is customary simply to issue warnings about "individualism" and wait for everyone else to nod wisely. But Robinson doesn't do this:

> I am praising that famous individualism associated with Western and American myth. When I praise anything, I proceed from the assumption that the distinctions available to us in this world are not arrayed between good and bad but between bad and worse. Tightly knit communities in which members look to one another for identity, and to establish meaning and value, are disabled and often dangerous, however polished their veneer. The opposition frequently made between individualism on the one hand and responsibility to society on the other is a false opposition, as we all know.[18]

When you walk up into the hills, into the high lonesome, you are not walking into autonomy. That is not how the individual is defined. When you walk into the town, you are not being swallowed by the hive. Advocates for either approach might define the alternative in this way, but the myth that Robinson is talking about here is more nuanced than that. So lonesome is not an absolute good; simply a relative one. Here, as elsewhere, Robinson's thought takes an unexpected turn, and the results are usually edifying.

However, I do offer one important criticism. Like many conservatives, I have been able to enjoy Robinson's writing, even though she appears to be quite at home in the liberal mainline tradition. Despite the differences I have had with her outlook on many issues, her novels are written with such depth, nuance, and sensitivity that it is easy to simply enjoy them. This is apparently because she sets her novels at or near the 1950s, back when all those characteristics were still legal.

In *Gilead* and *Home*, when Ames and Broughton have their periodic political "fusses," the first thing you see in and through the portrait she paints is their humanity. You see how the issues are complicated and how good people get themselves tangled up in very complex things. You see this in her treatment of the civil rights unrest in Montgomery, and you see it in her treatment of the Civil War—in the flashbacks in *Gilead* about Ames's father and grandfather and in the tensions between radicalism and pacifism. In her novels, some of the characters *have* demons, but none of them *are* demons. She creates absolutely no cartoons.

But it is plain to me that Robinson would be clearly incapable of writing a first-rate novel, of the same kind as these, set in the present time. In a recent interview with Religion News Service, she spoke in some very skewed and unflattering ways about people she clearly doesn't understand at all.[19] In this regard, she has a prophetic eye, but it is pressed to the keyhole of a very small room. She is a blinkered prophetess.

In that interview, she discusses conservative Christians, and it is astounding—given how she writes her novels—to find nothing *but* cartoons. Think of an evangelical NRA dad on a sitcom for CBS—that level. Christians want to carry a gun because they are "scared of the world." Opposition to same-sex mirage is an "old issue," and there will come a time when we will stop "calling down brimstone." Opposition to homosexuality based on the Old Testament, she says, shipwrecks on the modern practice of "eating oysters." Those who think this way are "primitive." Well, color me Ooog. She says that pro-life Christians are all about "babies that don't exist yet" and are "so negligent of babies that need help."

Now it would be easy to get distracted here and go charging off to answer the cartoon critique. That would be easy enough to do, but it would really miss what is happening. What we have here is a spectacular crash of a literary imagination, one that is capable of flying really high.

But this is a blind spot, not blindness. She plainly knows too much to not know how it works.

> We all know about hubris. We know that pride goeth before a fall. The problem is that we don't recognize pride or hubris in ourselves, any more than Oedipus did, any more than Job's so-called comforters. It can be so innocuous-seeming a thing as confidence that one is right, is competent, is clear-sighted, or confidence that one is pious or pure in one's motives.[20]

At the end of the interview, she is asked about Twitter and Facebook, and she responded more revealingly than she knew. She said, "I'd have to educate myself about what contemporary culture is, because all of these words are essentially meaningless to me. . . . So I might as well just write about 1956." I think this is very wise, but she also needs to have limited herself to interviews about the issues that were raging in 1956. She has no more idea of what pro-life adoptive parents who vote against the welfare state are like than she has of Facebook "Like" buttons.

Liberalism had its genesis in a failure of imagination, and as it has gone increasingly to seed, it has become progressively hostile to imagination, which includes the ability to place yourself in circumstances not your own—to feel through nerve endings not your own. In the early days of liberalism, this was an insular and provincial approach. Sometimes it was cute. As William F. Buckley once put it, "Liberals claim to want to give a hearing to other views, but then are shocked and offended to discover that there are other views."[21] But as the intolerance intrinsic to liberalism has grown stronger, we now have a mania that results in the phenomenon of other views getting shouted down, run out of business, or packed off to sensitivity training. One writer has coined quite a descriptive word for it—*totalitolerance*.

But Robinson is a holdover from the early days. She is an NPR liberal, not an intolerista liberal. She is a nice lady in a mainstream Congregational church and apparently doesn't get out much, at least not in the present time. She has had a failure of imagination here, which I would not rank as a full-fledged rebellion against it. Neither one is praiseworthy, of course, and her failure here *is* culpable. But in her case it is also ironic and contradictory. She is a very astute woman who is failing to be astute. It is like Wendell Berry that time, champion of *natural*, signing off on mainstreaming unnatural homosexual acts. It is like watching Fred Astaire joining in on a line dance.

So as it turns out, her abilities in cross-cultural empathy are limited. Conservative Christians who want to continue to appreciate her writing probably need to do it at a distance. Meeting her, and having an actual conversation, might burst the bubble she lives in. Or, as one person responded to me on this point, she might have the ability to recognize all the human complications and contributions in a conservative Christian she met, one who happened to be her next-door neighbor, but simply chalk it up as an exception. In her historical writing, she is able to see certain characters of this type as fully representative of a kind. But not here.

What is sad about this in her case is that she has been peculiarly gifted by God with an imagination. When she exercises her impulses of imaginative and sympathetic charity—as she is able to do with John Calvin, for instance—she excels. But with modern-day heirs of Calvin, not so much.

But enough with the criticism. Here we may return to our earlier praise of her writing, simply stated, without qualification. I believe the word used for this in politics is *pivot*. Here is an example of her large-minded approach to much-despised figures in church history, an approach that is striking in being both courageous and wise:

> Contrary to entrenched assumptions, contrary to the conventional associations made with the words "Calvinist" and "Puritan," and despite the fact that certain fairly austere communities can claim a heritage in Reformed culture and history,

Calvinism is uniquely the *fons et origo* of Christian liberalism in the modern period, that is, in the period since the Reformation, and this liberalism has had its origins largely in the Old Testament.[22]

This occurs in an essay called "Open Thy Hand Wide," and in it she piles outrage on top of outrage. The fountainhead of modern liberal generosity, she argues, is found in the Old Testament, recovered by John Calvin, and implemented widely by the Puritans. Not only does she argue this, but she argues it compellingly.

She sees how *tender* Deuteronomy is to the poor and to the debtor, and she sees it in contrast to how other ancient societies handled their poor. She uses words like *tender* and *haunting solicitude*. She also notes that those who had great reputations for broadmindedness did not always compare well with the religiously devout. She urges us to compare the Liberties of Puritan Massachusetts to the Grand Model for North Carolina, drawn up by John Locke in 1663, and which would have "established landed aristocracy and virtual feudalism in that colony."[23] By way of contrast, the Massachusetts Liberties don't even "mention property crime as a capital offense."[24]

In his conclusion to *An Experiment in Criticism*, C. S. Lewis says this:

> But in reading great literature I become a thousand men and yet remain myself. Like the night sky in the Greek poem, I see with a myriad eyes, but it is still I who see. Here, as in worship, in love, in moral action, and in knowing, I transcend myself; and am never more myself than when I do.[25]

Robinson has an amazing ability to enable readers to do just that. When I was reading *Gilead*, I was astounded at Robinson's ability to write in the first person, and to have the narrator be an elderly man, a pastor, reflecting on many years of ministry. The things I was familiar with rang true, and the things she introduced to me rang just as true. It was magnificent.

IF YOU READ NOTHING ELSE

Robinson's books are not numerous, so they could certainly all be read easily if you like, but if time and resources are limited, I recommend making a particular point of reading *Gilead* and *Home*. Her first novel, *Housekeeping*, was eerie and grim. It was fun for me though, in an odd kind of way, because, as I mentioned, the whole thing was set in a fictional part of northern Idaho, right close to where I live. She did a wonderful job in describing it, but it was still gray granite, polished to shine with a high luster.

With *Gilead* and *Home* she pulled off a remarkable feat by telling the same story in two different books, writing from two different angles. A third novel about Gilead, *Lila*, written from the perspective of yet another of the characters, is sure to add to the texture of the whole thing. I am sure I will read it, but the deadline for this manuscript means I am not really in a position to comment on it now.

For those who would like to try their hand at her nonfiction, I would recommend *When I Was a Child I Read Books*. This is a collection on various topics and is not nearly as heady as her *Absence of Mind*.

N. D. Wilson

Meaningless Disclaimer: It will not have escaped the notice of many readers that the subject of this chapter is my son, Nathan Wilson. For some this will mean that my observations will be hopelessly subjective, and for others it will mean that I will be writing from a vantage point on the fifty-yard line that has some singular advantages. As is the case in many of these complicated situations, everybody has a point. But in writing a book like this, it would have been really difficult to go on about C. S. and P. G. and T. S. and G. K. without also adding something about N. D. In some important respects, Nate's writing is, at least in my view, a culmination of the work done by many of these other writers. And if the suggestion is made—as it quite possibly might be—that I am including him alongside all these other worthies out of a paternal desire to puff him up into authorial importance, I would reply that any efforts of mine in that department would be both vain and superfluous. His *Cupboards* has sold about three-quarters of a million copies in North America and has been translated into about twenty languages. So I am actually commenting here on something that has happened and am not trying to get it to happen.

A WRITER'S LIFE

Nathan David Wilson was named after the prophet who delivered the rebuke and the king who received it. He was born in 1978 in Moscow, Idaho. He is our middle child and only son. He has an older sister Bekah (Merkle) and a younger sister Rachel (Jankovic). The three of them were close enough in age to travel in a pack much of the time, and because they all still live here in Moscow, the sixteen cousins travel in a much larger pack. There is a great deal of cousin action.

He might want to modify some of this or explain it differently, but from the vantage point of his mother and me, there were three major influences on the aspect of his soul that was open to the power and influence of stories. The first came from his grandparents on both sides, particularly his grandfathers. They were full of stories, and they were willing to tell them. There were war stories, sea stories, and evangelism stories. One time when Nate was a very young boy, my father took a trip around the world to minister to straying missionary kids. When he came back, he had so many stories to tell that we organized an event so that he wouldn't have to tell the stories over and over again. When we were leaving, Nate, who was about two, told us, "when I grow up, I want to be like Grandpa and tell people about my trip."

The second influence was the presence of books and stories read aloud in our home. I had grown up in a home full of books, and my father would regularly and routinely read to us—from as far back as I can remember. After I was grown and gone from home, my father could still fill up his living room with college students in order to read them stories from *Winnie the Pooh*. In my thinking, this was just something people did. And so we did the same kind of thing for our children. Reading aloud was simply part of the atmosphere of the home. When the kids were little, I would lie down on the couch, book held over my upper chest, and the children would sit all over the rest of me. It was not exactly ergonomic, but it was still great fun. The first time we read *The Lord of the Rings* that way, Nate was about two. It didn't seem possible to us that he could be tracking with it, but he sat still like a stone. One time during a battle scene, Nancy came over and touched his cheek, and it was hot. He was listening, all right.

The third element was our involvement in the establishment of Logos School. Even creative writer types need to have their metaphorical knuckles rapped by a schoolmarm using the yardstick of grammar, and they also need to be restricted by and interfered with through the unreasonable expectations of other people not related to them. There was the discipline of Latin in elementary school, there was the rigorous logic of the dialectic stage, but most of all there were the good stories found in the classics. I recall one evening at dinner. We were all faithfully eating, and Nate was holding our attention by retelling us stories out of Herodotus while his food got cold. It wasn't all strawberries and cream though. I remember that some teacher one time, somehow, for some reason, had the class read *Babbitt*. I have never seen a young man hate a book as much as Nate hated that book. He had opinions about it, and I believe that he must have sworn an oath on the altar of his ancestors to write as many unBabbitts as he could.

The school was very young when Nate first started out in kindergarten, and it was therefore quite small as compared to now. His mother and I prayed that God would bring him a friend. In answer to that prayer, as the school grew, Joe Casebolt joined him in second grade. Some of Nate's early experiences with barns and packing-foam rafts in creeks, which showed up later in *100 Cupboards* and *Leepike Ridge*, happened out at the Casebolt place. Nate and Joe are currently serving together on the Logos School board, having different kinds of adventures now, with more budgets and fewer makeshift rafts.

He graduated from Logos School in 1996. He began dual-track enrollment at the University of Idaho and New St. Andrews together, but after one academic travesty too many at the UI—on the university's side, not his—he transferred over to NSA full time. The quality of poor instruction at UI was epic, but the reason he had stuck it out as long as he did was that he wanted to play Division I basketball. He had tried out in order to walk on the team and had not heard back from the coach when the academic jokes that were his classes got to the point of critical mass. He and I talked about him transferring over to NSA and just being done with the UI. This was a striking occasion for both of us in learning to "read the story you are in." I told him that it was fine with me if he did that, but he needed to know that as soon he came over to NSA solely, he was going to get a call from the coach, inviting him to play basketball. He told me he knew that, but it wasn't worth it. He said that his Logos education prepared him for the fight but that this wasn't fighting. He said it was more like tearing apart a stress doll. And sure enough, within a week or so of transferring, he got a call from the coach. Many thanks for the offer, but he was attending another school now.

Upon transferring to NSA, he finished in three years, graduating in 1999. Because of NSA's accreditation status at the time (since addressed by TRACS), getting into grad school was a challenge. He wound up attending Liberty University for the first year of his MA and finishing out at St. John's College in Annapolis.

He had met Heather Garaway in the course of his last year in grad school, and they married in April of 2001. She was from Santa Cruz and was a sponsored professional surfer. Goes to show that you shouldn't be too confident about what's going to happen next. In the years since, they have been graced with five children—a datum of astonishment to the people that Nate works with in the New York publishing world. They have two sons, Rory and Seamus, and three daughters, Lucia, Ameera, and Marisol—and all together they are quite a happy clan. The Christmas just prior to this writing, they added a German shorthaired pointer named Dixie Mist. This was the fourth member of the animal kingdom added to their collection of fauna; they already had a snake named Jack and two huge tortoises named Rosalinda and Tasha. The tortoises are long-lived, incidentally, and so provisions will have to be made in somebody's will as to which of their grandchildren get them. They will also be cumbersome by that point, about the size of a hassock.

After grad school, Nate and Heather returned to Moscow, where he began to teach part-time at New St. Andrews and settled into the serious business of trying to make it as a writer. His Left Behind spoofs were published by Canon Press, but he didn't really crack into the business until Random House acquired *Leepike Ridge* and another monster book that was reworked into the 100 Cupboards trilogy. That came about, in part, because Nate had teamed up with Aaron Rench, a college friend from NSA, who was breaking into the literary agent business at around the same time. Nate was for all intents and purposes a first-time author, and Aaron was a first-time agent, but they nevertheless landed a really good arrangement with Random House. Someone close to the publishing business told them that he hoped they recognized that this kind of thing never, ever happens.

Another significant splash happened during grad school when Nate found a milestone alongside the lake and threw it in the water. He had had an instructor in grad school who was big into the Shroud of Turin as an important part of his apologetic for Christianity. This bothered Nate greatly because the scriptural account of Christ's graveclothes says that they came in two pieces instead of a single shroud that covers both front and back. It couldn't be genuine, but it *had* to be remarkable. The shroud goes back to medieval times and yet is a photo-negative image of a man before such things existed, and on top of that, the image renders into 3-D. If it is a fraud, then we have to explain how a fraud could be almost as remarkable as the image of a miraculous resurrection.

During the time this particular burr was under his saddle, Nancy gave Nate a collection of Father Brown stories by Chesterton for Christmas. Having steeped himself in them, he was home on break and sat on his hands for a long time in our living room. What he did, in brief, was drop the mystery of the shroud into a Father Brown story in order to let Chesterton solve it. And since the mystery concerned how that image could possibly have gotten onto the cloth, Nate's line of reasoning made perfect sense—the image wasn't put on the cloth. Everything that wasn't the image was taken off. So Nate got a *dark* piece of linen, took a hand-painted image of Jesus on glass, and set it out in the sun. The sun bleached the exposed linen, creating a photo negative, and the sun traveled in an arc over it, like a giant MRI, creating a 3-D image, and all with technology available in medieval times. The results of this remarkable experiment were printed in *Books & Culture* magazine under the title "Father Brown Fakes the Shroud." A few years later, Nate was doing a special for *National Geographic* on the subject, and his shroud was given a few more tests by another shroud researcher in Italy, and passed. His shroud is a genuine fake, in other words.

DIGGING DEEPER

One of the themes that runs throughout Nate's books is that of dealing with fatherlessness fruitfully. And this means that you must deal with missing fathers by *finding* fathers. You don't do it by jerry-rigging a false alternative. You don't do it by proving that fathers are superfluous.

In *Leepike Ridge* Tom Hammond's father has been dead for three years, and he is living together with his mother. In *100 Cupboards* Henry York is growing up with a man who isn't his father, and they never connect the way a father and a son should. He finds out the reason for this, much to his relief, in the course of the story. In his adventures on the other side of the cupboard doors, he finds his true-home world and his true father. In the Ashtown series, Cyrus and his siblings have to deal with the fact that their mother is in a coma and their father is dead. As the story unfolds, they actually have an opportunity to bring their father back from the dead—but unlawfully—and they resist the temptation. Their need for a father is met by quite an admirable man named Rupert Greeves. In *Boys of Blur* a stepfather is the needed father, while the true father eventually returns for a final act of fatherly protection.

This scenario in *Boys of Blur* is actually unusual in Nate's writing; usually the father is absent, but not in a way that would create shame in a boy. A boy whose father died heroically in a war is in a very different place from a boy whose father deserted him by deserting his mother. Both boys have to deal with the absence, but the way it is dealt with is different.

And this relates to another feature of the kind of fiction in which children have "incredible adventures." In order to have those incredible adventures, responsible adults usually have to be out of the picture, but they have to be out of the picture in a way that doesn't make the adults seem amazingly irresponsible. The Pevensie children have to be able to get into Narnia without our taking a very dim view of their parents.

In his nonfiction Nate touches on this same theme in another way. In *Notes from the Tilt-a-Whirl* the fatherhood of God lies behind everything. This apparent chaotic world is not chaotic at all; if we step back and take it all in with the right perspective, we see that it is an intricately designed carnival ride. There is a fatherly purpose in it: it turns out that we thought we were being born into a world full of sound and fury, signifying nothing, but what was happening is that our Father was taking us to a particularly spectacular fair with some really gnarly rides.

In *Death by Living* Nate spends a great deal of time honoring his two grandfathers, in turn, my wife's father, Larry Greensides, now with the Lord, and my own father, Jim Wilson. And, as Paul mentions in Ephesians (3:14–15), behind all such admirable fathers is the Father. All fatherhood derives its name from the Father of all things. The heart of wisdom is to learn to see the Father in earthly fathers and not be distracted by their sins and failings. The Father is much more like they are than they are themselves (Heb. 12:11). The window might be dirty because of sin, but we all still need to see through it.

Behind and through all of this is a robust understanding of fatherhood at the source of everything. If we lived in a fatherless cosmos, then little outbreaks of fatherhood here and there would simply be small insanities. In a random universe, everything is random. Fatherhood here and/or there would be just another random event. Fatherhood would be just as random as fatherlessness. But if we live in a world where the Father is behind and beneath everything, then every true adventure has to consist of finding our way back to that place, overcoming the obstacles that came about as a result of estrangement from the Father. Those obstacles are placed by sin and rebellion, and so finding the Father is the archetypal adventure. This is the central reason why Nate's books work as effectively as they do.

One great theme in literature is the comedic theme, with the story ending in a wedding. This is reflective of the reality of Christ's mission to earth, to seek out and win his bride, which is what we see him doing in his death and resurrection. It is the archetype of the St. George adventure—rescue the princess by killing the dragon. My friend Joe Rigney has this as a tagline on the bottom of every e-mail: "Kill the dragon, get the girl." That is the point of human history, and so we brought it over into our celebration of the Lord's Day. It is something I have my grandchildren say to me every week at our sabbath dinner: "Kids, what's the point of the whole Bible?" "*Kill the dragon, get the girl!*" This is the point of everything.

But even a great story like that needs to have a foundational story underneath it. The doctrine of the atonement depends upon the doctrine of the incarnation. The knight may kill the dragon in order to rescue the princess, and so it is a basic story. But there is a story before it. We need a father who sent his son out to accomplish the mission. Before the knight wins his fair lady, we need to have a father who has a faithful son. So stories about reconciliations or reunions with fathers tap into something very powerful indeed.

Another strong element and theme in Nate's writing might be called "regained perspective." Most of his books are fantasy literature, but what does that actually mean? Tolkien once chided those who objected to fantasy literature as "escapist." He said that we have a name for people who don't like escape—we call them jailers. Everything turns on what we are escaping *from* and what we are escaping *to*. A central device of Nate's writing is to enable the reader to escape from the world in order to escape into it. In this, his goal is fundamentally Chestertonian. In *Manalive* the main character, Innocent Smith, runs away from his life in order to discover it anew. In *Orthodoxy* Chesterton compares himself to a man who thought he was discovering a new island, but when he landed, turns out it was actually England. Browning's poem "Fra Lippo Lippi" makes the point that a painter's task is to capture an image, not so that we might then possess that image but so that we might see the thing that was painted with fresh eyes. C. S. Lewis says it this way:

> If you are tired of the real landscape, look at it in a mirror. By putting bread, gold, horse, apple, or the very roads into a myth, we do not retreat from reality, we rediscover it. As long as the story lingers in our mind, the real things are more themselves. . . . By dipping them in myth, we see them more clearly.[1]

Nate's fantasy novels take the children out of their humdrum world, not so that they might escape from the humdrummery, but so that they might learn that this world is every bit as marvelous as the one they have gotten themselves into. And in his nonfiction, he makes the same point by describing ordinary things in extraordinary terms:

> I live on a near perfect sphere hurtling through space at around 67,000 miles per hour. Mach 86 to you pilots. Of course, this sphere of mine is also spinning while it hurtles, so tack on an extra 1,000 miles per hour at the fat parts. And it's all tucked into this giant hurricane of stars.[2]

The point, of course, is to state what we all learned in the unfolding of our basic science education but to do so in a way that makes it apparent that we all must have devised a way to forget what we were learning at the very moment we were learning it. The trick is to state what we know in a recognizable fashion but in a way that is slightly off, in a way that *arrests* us. It is like the trick we used to play on ourselves as children, when we would hang off the couch in the living room and look at the whole thing upside down. There was all the old familiar stuff but completely inverted. We were entirely at home, recognizing everything, and yet everything was new.

Speaking of this same peculiar gift that Chesterton had, Dale Ahlquist says this: "He says that he knows there should be priests to remind men that they will one day die. But there should also be another kind of priest to remind men that they are not dead yet."[3]

Not dead yet. And if you are not dead yet, it is a great blessing to have writers who prod you and who point that out. If we are not dead yet, shouldn't we be noticing more life than we do?

> Dandelions were not magic. They couldn't be. They were here. They were normal. You couldn't shut them up someplace or even keep them out of your lawn. If they were magic, well, then everything was.[4]

Another characteristic of all Nate's writing, whether nonfiction or fiction, and related to the previous point, is that in reading, sensations come in at you through every pore. His writing is vivid, and it comes at you from every direction. Many writers settle for one sensation at a time, but not Nate.

One easy groove for writers to slip into is to "pick a sense" and work it. The protagonist walks into a room, and the writer describes for us how it looks. Or perhaps he describes a cacophonous noise from the alley outside, or how a house smells. It is as though one sensual experience is out there for a protagonist to walk into. In Nate's writing, in his fiction particularly, the sensations are going on inside the protagonist and with the reader right in there with him. This provides an unusual level of story grip. Here is an example from *Dandelion Fire*:

> Henry was cold. Very cold. His pants were wet and clinging to his legs. His blood had been replaced with frigid water, and greasy coils of brown rope were digging into his cheek. His eyes seemed to be working again, but not well. He tried to push himself up, but his hands were tied behind his back. The floor was

rising and falling beneath him, and he could feel water puddling and spilling around his stomach and legs.[5]

Sensory experience should not be draped on top of the story as sort of a last-minute decoration. Done right, it is woven into the fabric of the story, and as this happens, the reader is woven in, right alongside the description. In giving advice to writers, E. L. Doctorow once said that good writing should communicate more than the mere fact that it is raining. The reader should feel rained on.

A fourth issue has to do with courage. C. S. Lewis pointed out somewhere that courage is not a separate virtue but is rather the testing point of all the virtues: "Sometimes standing against evil is more important than defeating it. The greatest heroes stand because it is right to do so, not because they believe they will walk away with their lives."[6] In novels with cartoon virtue, courage is simple and scarcely even necessary. In novels with no virtue, there is no point—everything is gritty and gray. In novels that do what stories like this ought to do, you keep going when you don't think you can, like Shasta running. You are afraid, and you do the right thing anyway. Utter fearlessness is not human courage. Complete despair comes to those who are abandoning what it means to be created in the image of God. Courage is the only alternative.

But, of course, if men are to be courageous, boys must learn to be courageous. If women are to be women of courage, then that is something they learn at some point. What we are when grown is what we learned to be while we were still growing. But while we are learning this, we are trying to grasp the unfamiliar. This is why stories like this, with great evils in them, are necessary for children to read. Kids just got here—they are still figuring things out, and stories are one of the central realities that can help them. Chesterton says somewhere that stories about dragons and knights do not teach children to fear dragons. They had dragons under the bed already. They had the fear *already*. The stories actually teach children that dragons can be killed.

And last, we have to look at all the allusive things that never quite take center stage. Behind and underneath Nate's stories there are a host of oblique stories and obscure legends, barely referred to, but which enterprising readers can certainly chase down if they have a mind to (and if it occurs to them). Just a few examples should suffice. A number of the names in *Leepike Ridge* are meant to make the reader think of the Odyssey—from Argus the dog, to Nestor, to Lotus. Nobody remembers who Pook is supposed to be, though. And at the end of that same book, the stupendous Chinese treasure they find in North America might be that of Admiral Cheng. Or perhaps it was left there by Fu Hsi, the Chinese Noah, tamer of the animals. The back stories throughout Nate's books have back walls, and they have doors in them. Kids should explore them more. Not only should more houses have secret passageways; more stories ought to. Not only do his stories have cupboards in them; they also have cupboards in *them*.

In *Boys of Blur* the story depends on Grendels—or Stanks— haunting the swamps of Florida. And there is a passing reference to Ponce De Leon and his Fountain of Youth, located in that same vicinity. But you have to be paying attention; otherwise you might miss it. The affable villain of the Ashtown series is Ben Sterling, with two prosthetic legs, upping Long John Silver by one artificial leg. And Sterling might make you think of Silver, if you were watching closely. And the central protagonists in that series are named Cyrus and Antigone, which should make you wish you had paid closer attention in your history and lit classes.

So the takeaway impact is this. I have a Father, this world is my home even if I look at it sideways—*especially* if I look at it sideways—and this world is meant to be *lived* in. The world around us is marinade, and we need to be submerged in it. But living in it requires that we take stock of it, and when we do, we find that there are adversaries to overcome. Doing so might cost us something, but what we receive in return is fullness of life. When we begin to live in that fullness, it is not long before we realize that everything is connected—the *real* world is honeycombed with secret passages.

IF YOU READ NOTHING ELSE

The books that Nate has written thus far are these. He began his life in print with two spoofs of the Left Behind series. The first was *Right Behind* (2001), followed up by *Supergeddon* (2003)—a Really Big Geddon. His first real novel was *Leepike Ridge* (2007). That was followed by the Cupboards trilogy: *100 Cupboards* (2007); *Dandelion Fire* (2009); and *The Chestnut King* (2010). The next fantasy series is called The Ashtown Burials, beginning with *The Dragon's Tooth* (2011); then *The Drowned Vault* (2012); and then *Empire of Bones* (2013). This series will finish out with a fourth book, as yet unwritten and unnamed. One more stand-alone novel is called *Boys of Blur* (2014). His nonfiction work consists of *Notes from the Tilt-a-Whirl* (2009) and *Death by Living* (2013). Bringing up the rear are two board books for little children: *Hello Ninja* (2013) and *Blah Blah Black Sheep* (2013). In short, if you act quickly and do it now, you can get through his entire corpus. His infamous article for *Books & Culture* on the Shroud of Turin was titled "Father Brown Fakes the Shroud," which is now available as a booklet from Canon Press (2014).

Afterword

So, if you would heed my suggestion, these are writers you really should read. These obviously are not the *only* writers you should read, but they are a wonderful place to begin. I love them all, and at least four of them are woven into the fabric of my thoughts in ways that I could not begin to recognize. I recognize, of course, that they are there, but I cannot fathom the ways in which they are.

If you love to read, you may already be jazzed enough to start. You believe that I have gone on quite long enough and are ready for this book to be done so that you can get to some writers who are really worth it.

But if the list looks simultaneously appealing and overwhelming to you, my suggestion is that you take it a piece at a time. I am a great believer in plodding. One time I agreed to review a book for a particular publication, and when it arrived in the mail, I discovered that it was a great whale of a book—seven hundred pages, I think. So I counted the number of days until the book review was due, backed off a couple of weeks for the writing, and got the number of days I had available for reading. I then divided the number of days into the number of pages and got how many pages I would have to read every day to be done in time. And that, more or less, is what I did. It is kind of amazing how fast this kind of thing adds up. Plodding does get you there.

If on this scheme you were to read Chesterton's *Orthodoxy* first, you would be done in sixteen days. If you picked up Mencken's *Chrestomathy* next, which is kind of big, you would be done with that in just over a couple of months. Then there would be Wode-house. You would start with *Leave It to Psmith* and would be thirty pages in after three days, and then you would finish it the next night. But don't do that too often. If you then moved on to Eliot's poetry, I would read the same number of pages, but go a little slower in order to be able to savor it. Or perhaps to say *huh?* to yourself. You get the idea.

When you meet a new friend, you should be willing for the blessings of that relationship to accumulate over a long period of time. It is the same here, and I trust they will be as good to you as they have been to me.

Notes

Chapter 1: G. K. Chesterton

1. Douglas Wilson, *Against the Church* (Moscow, ID: Canon Press, 2013), 53.
2. Thomas C. Peters, *The Christian Imagination: G.K. Chesterton on the Arts* (San Francisco: Ignatius, 2000), 35–36.
3. C. S. Lewis, *Mere Christianity* (New York: Collier, 1952), 175.
4. G. K. Chesterton, *Heretics* (New York: John Lane, 1909), 121.
5. G. K. Chesterton, *The Everlasting Man* (San Francisco: Ignatius, 1993), 153.
6. Christine Rosen, *Preaching Eugenics: Religious Leaders and the American Eugenics Movement* (Oxford: Oxford University Press, 2004), 147.
7. Kevin Belmonte, *The Quotable Chesterton: The Wit and Wisdom of G.K. Chesterton* (Nashville: Thomas Nelson, 2011), 267.
8. Ibid., 149.
9. Ibid., 16.
10. George Marlin, Richard P. Rabatin, and John L. Swan, *More Quotable Chesterton: A Topical Compilation of the Wit, Wisdom, and Satire of G.K. Chesterton* (San Francisco: Ignatius, 1988), 508.
11. Ibid., 351.
12. Ibid., 351–52.

Chapter 2: H. L. Mencken

1. Terry Teachout, *The Skeptic: A Life of H. L. Mencken* (New York: HarperCollins, 2002), 67.
2. H. L. Mencken, *The Gist of Mencken* (Metuchen, NJ: Scarecrow Press, 1990), 28.
3. H. L. Mencken, *My Life as Author and Editor* (New York: Knopf, 1992), viii.
4. Teachout, *The Skeptic*, 106.
5. Ibid., 75.
6. Ibid., 145.
7. Ibid., 168.

8. Ibid., *xi*.
9. Ibid., 15.
10. http://phillysoc.org/teachout-2004-national-meeting/.
11. H. L. Mencken, *Happy Days: Mencken's Autobiography*, Maryland Paperback Bookshelf (Baltimore, MD: Johns Hopkins University Press, 1996), *xi*.
12. Ibid., *xiii*.
13. H. L. Mencken, *A Mencken Chrestomathy* (New York: Random House, 1949), 17.
14. Aubrey Dillon-Malone, "Morley," *The Cynic's Dictionary* (Chicago: Contemporary Books, 2000), 64.
15. Ibid., "Tynan," n.p.
16. Ibid., "Behan," n.p.
17. Marvin Olasky, *Prodigal Press: The Anti-Christian Bias of the American News Media* (Westchester, IL: Crossway, 1988), 59–71.
18. John Burroughs, cited in *The Bookman* (October 1908): 60.
19. Mencken, *Chrestomathy*, 13–14.
20. Cited in Gary North, *Westminster's Confession: The Abandonment of Van Til's Legacy* (Tyler, TX: Institute for Christian Economics, 1991) 312–13.
21. Ibid.
22. Mencken, *Chrestomathy*, 620.

Chapter 3: P. G. Wodehouse

1. Cited in Steven D. Price, *The Little Black Book of Writers' Wisdom* (New York: Skyhorse, 2013), 33.
2. P. G. Wodehouse, *P. G. Wodehouse: A Life in Letters* (New York: Norton, 2011), 325.
3. P. G. Wodehouse, *Just Enough Jeeves* (New York: Norton, 2010), 300.
4. Robert McCrum, *Wodehouse: A Life* (New York: Norton, 2004), 172.
5. John Broadus, *A Treatise on the Preparation and Delivery of Sermons* (Philadelphia: Nelson S. Quiney, 1882), 324.
6. C. S. Lewis, *Surprised by Joy* (New York: Harcourt, Brace, & World, 1955), 190–91.

Chapter 4: T. S. Eliot

1. Thomas Howard, *Dove Descending: A Journey into T. S. Eliot's Four Quartets* (San Francisco: Ignatius, 2006), 15.
2. C. S. Lewis, *A Preface to Paradise Lost* (Oxford: Oxford University Press, 1942), 137.
3. Ibid., 9.
4. C. S. Lewis, *Image and Imagination* (Cambridge, UK: Cambridge University Press, 2013), 137.
5. T. S. Eliot, *Christianity and Culture* (New York: Harcourt Brace, 1976), 144.
6. Ibid., 101.

7. Ibid., 127.
8. Ibid., 196.
9. Howard, *Dove Descending*, 23.
10. Kathryn Lindskoog, *Finding the Landlord: A Guide to C. S. Lewis's Pilgrim's Regress* (Chicago: Cornerstone Press, 1995), 61.
11. Howard, *Dove Descending*, 16.
12. Ibid., 41.
13. Ibid.
14. C. S. Lewis, "Donne and Love Poetry" [1938], in *Selected Literary Essays* (Cambridge, UK: Cambridge University Press, 1979), 116.
15. Peter Matheson, *The Imaginative World of the Reformation* (Minneapolis: Fortress Press, 2001), 8.
16. Lewis, *Image and Imagination*, 163–64.
17. Robert Daly, *God's Altar* (Berkeley, CA: University of California Press, 1978), 222.
18. Peter Leithart, *Ascent to Love: A Guide to Dante's Divine Comedy* (Moscow, ID: Canon Press, 2001), 76.
19. Cited in *1001 Quotations That Connect*, ed. Craig Brian Larson and Brian Lowrey (Grand Rapids, MI: Zondervan, 2009), quotation 408.
20. As quoted in Thomas C. Peters, *The Christian Imagination: G. K. Chesterton on the Arts* (San Francisco: Ignatius, 2000), 94–95.
21. Ibid.
22. Eliot, *Christianity and Culture*, 116.
23. T. S. Eliot, *On Poetry and Poets* (New York: Noonday Press, 1957), 7.
24. Ibid., 8.
25. Ibid.
26. Ibid.
27. Ibid., 15.
28. Ibid., 11.
29. Ibid., 10–11.

Chapter 5: J. R. R. Tolkien

1. Humphrey Carpenter, *Tolkien: The Authorized Biography* (New York: Ballantine, 1977), 54.
2. C. S. Lewis, *All My Road Before Me* (New York: Harcourt, Brace, 1991), 393.
3. Quoted in Carpenter, *Tolkien*, 161.
4. C. S. Lewis, *Image and Imagination* (Cambridge, UK: Cambridge University Press, 2013), 96.
5. Carpenter, *Tolkien*, 165.
6. Ibid., 168.
7. C. S. Lewis, *English Literature in the Sixteenth Century* (Oxford, UK: Oxford University Press, 1954), 40.
8. Ibid., 37.
9. Ibid., 33.

10. C. S. Lewis, *Letters of C. S. Lewis*, rev. ed., ed. Walter Hooper (Eugene, OR: Harvest, 1993), 406.
11. J. R. R. Tolkien, *The Letters of J. R. R. Tolkien*, ed. Humphrey Carpenter (New York: Houghton Mifflin, 2000), 72.
12. Ibid., 41.
13. Ibid., 145.
14. Ibid., 121.
15. C. S. Lewis, *The Allegory of Love* (Oxford, UK: Oxford University Press, 1936), 60.
16. Ibid., 52.
17. Ibid., 45.
18. Lewis, *Letters*, 475.
19. C. S. Lewis, *Surprised by Joy* (New York: Harcourt, Brace, & World, 1955), 7.
20. Ibid., 16.
21. Ibid., 17.
22. Lewis, *Image and Imagination*, 100.
23. Tolkien, *Letters of J. R. R. Tolkien*, 92.
24. Ibid., 21.
25. Ibid., 144–45.
26. Ibid., 212.
27. Ibid., 376.
28. Ibid., 55–56.
29. J. R. R. Tolkien, *The Monsters and the Critics* (London: HarperCollins, 1997), 13.
30. Ibid., 20–21.
31. Ibid., 22.
32. Tolkien, *Letters of J. R. R. Tolkien*, 100.
33. C. S. Lewis, ed., *Essays Presented to Charles Williams* (Grand Rapids, MI: Eerdmans, 1966), 81.
34. Ibid., 84.
35. Lewis, *Image and Imagination*, 102.
36. Tolkien, *Letters of J. R. R. Tolkien*, 158.
37. Ibid., 189.
38. Ibid., 85.
39. Ibid., 149.
40. Ibid., 176, emphasis added.
41. Ibid., 178.
42. Ibid., 287, cf. 191.
43. Ibid., 190.
44. Lewis, *Image and Imagination*, 105.

Chapter 6: C. S. Lewis

1. C. S. Lewis, *Surprised by Joy* (New York: Harcourt, Brace, & World, 1955), 7.

2. Ibid., 16–17.
3. Ibid., 17.
4. C. S. Lewis, *The Weight of Glory and Other Addresses* (Grand Rapids, MI: Eerdmans, 1965), 13, emphasis original.
5. C. S. Lewis, *Christian Reflections* (Grand Rapids, MI: Eerdmans, 1967), 72–81.
6. Lewis, *Surprised by Joy*, 77.
7. Ibid., 144.
8. Ibid., 145.
9. Ibid., 179.
10. Ibid., 190–91. "God is, if I may say it, very unscrupulous" (191).
11. C. S. Lewis, "Imagination and Thought," in *Studies in Medieval and Renaissance Literature*, ed. Walter Hooper (Cambridge, UK: Cambridge University Press, 1966), 45.
12. Ibid., 47.
13. C. S. Lewis, *The Voyage of the Dawn Treader*, Chronicles of Narnia (New York: HarperCollins, 1952), 117.
14. Michael Ward, *Planet Narnia: The Seven Heavens in the Imagination of C. S. Lewis* (Oxford, UK: Oxford University Press, 2008), 1.
15. Douglas Wilson, *What I Learned in Narnia* (Moscow, ID: Canon Press, 2010), 9.
16. Ward, *Planet Narnia*, 16.
17. Ibid., 18.
18. Ibid., 75.
19. Lewis, *Surprised by Joy*, 7.
20. C. S. Lewis, *The Abolition of Man* (Toronto: Macmillan, 1969), 13.
21. Ibid., 17.
22. C. S. Lewis, "The Poison of Subjectivism," in *Christian Reflections*, 75.
23. Lewis, *Abolition*, 20.
24. Ibid., 24.
25. Lewis, "Poison of Subjectivism," 75.

Chapter 7: R. F. Capon

1. Robert Farrar Capon, *The Romance of the Word: One Man's Love Affair with Theology* (Grand Rapids, MI: Eerdmans, 1995), 2.
2. Ibid., 4.
3. Ibid.
4. Ibid., 4–5.
5. Ibid., 5.
6. Ibid.
7. Ibid.
8. Ibid.
9. http://donmilam.com/tag/radical-grace/.
10. Capon, *Romance of the Word*, 176–77.
11. Ibid., 19.

12. Ibid., 14.

13. Ibid.

14. Ibid., 26–27.

15. Robert Farrar Capon, *Kingdom, Grace, Judgment: Paradox, Outrage, and Vindication in the Parables of Jesus* (Grand Rapids, MI: Eerdmans, 2002), 365, emphasis original.

16. Ibid., 17.

17. Robert Farrar Capon, *The Supper of the Lamb: A Culinary Reflection* (New York: Smithmark, 1967), 123, emphasis original.

18. Ibid., 126.

19. Ibid., 150.

20. Ibid., 153.

21. Ibid., 8.

22. Ibid., 28.

23. Ibid., 19–20.

24. Ibid., 108.

25. Ibid., 40, emphasis original.

26. Ibid., 86.

27. Ibid., 180, emphasis original.

Chapter 8: M. S. Robinson

1. Marilyn Robinson, *When I Was a Child I Read Books: Essays* (New York: Picador, 2012), 86.

2. Ibid., *xiv*.

3. Ibid., 85.

4. Ibid., 4.

5. Ibid., 4–5.

6. Ibid., 6.

7. Ibid., 6, emphasis original.

8. Stephen King, *On Writing: A Memoir of the Craft* (New York: Scribner, 2000), 82.

9. Robinson, *When I Was a Child*, xi, emphasis added.

10. Ibid., *ix*, emphasis added.

11. Ibid., 91.

12. Ibid., 90.

13. Marilyn Robinson, *Housekeeping* (New York: Picador, 1980), 15.

14. Ibid., 65.

15. Ibid., 112.

16. Ibid., 98.

17. Robinson, *When I Was a Child*, 88.

18. Ibid., 90.

19. http://www.religionnews.com/2014/05/09/qa-marilynne-robinson-guns-gay-marriage-calvinism/.

20. Robinson, *When I Was a Child*, 17.

21. Cited in Jeffrey Peter Hart, *The American Dissent: A Decade of Modern Conservatism* (New York: Doubleday, 1966), 171.

22. Robinson, *When I Was a Child*, 64.
23. Ibid., 74.
24. Ibid.
25. C. S. Lewis, *An Experiment in Criticism* (Cambridge, UK: Cambridge University Press, 1969), 141.

Chapter 9: N. D. Wilson

1. C. S. Lewis, *Image and Imagination* (Cambridge, UK: Cambridge University Press, 2013), 108.
2. N. D. Wilson, *Notes from the Tilt-a-Whirl* (Nashville: Thomas Nelson, 2009), 2.
3. Dale Ahlquist, *Common Sense 101: Lessons from G. K. Chesterton* (San Francisco: Ignatius Press, 2006), 228.
4. N. D. Wilson, *Dandelion Fire* (New York: Random House, 2009), 66.
5. Ibid., 263.
6. Just for grins, I will cite this quote from *Dandelion Fire* as it was quoted in an article on courage in *Psychology Today*, http://www.psychologytoday.com/blog/the-mindful-self-express/201208/the-six-attributes-courage.

Index